The
Four
Faces
of Man

A Philosophical Study
of Practice,
Reason, Art, and
Religion

The
Four
Irwin C. Lieb Faces
# of Man

―

University of Pennsylvania Press

Philadelphia

Contents

Preface

This essay returns to a theme in classical philosophy—the kinds of men we are and the kinds of lives we lead. For a long while, we have not explored this theme with care. There are many causes for its neglect, but two moods of thought seem to stand out from the rest. The first of these—many of us share in it—is that we simply do not know enough, we are still too ignorant, to talk about men in general. We have impressions, of course; we are often moved by the compelling pictures set before us in the arts; but to come to good confidence about the truth in general, many of us feel that we have still to wait, perhaps for a long while.

The second mood which keeps us from asking about the kinds of men we are is opposite from the first. It is simply that we already know the basic truth about ourselves—that human nature is seamless and in everyone the same. There is a single human nature; there are no deeply different kinds. The so-called kinds are artificial, superficial, revealing nothing of what we really are.

Preface

Besides, these are times when we should emphasize the sameness of all men and not play on surface differences.

These—disabling ignorance and surfeit knowledge—have been the main two tempers which have made us disinclined to ask what kinds of men we are. Neither, however, should have its force, for neither is altogether sound.

Take the first: of course reliable general knowledge depends on wide learning and long experience. But it is a mistake to think that very general ideas are a summary of specific facts. They are connected with facts in a much different way, for even to count something as a fact, we have to know the general ideas which are specified in it; they explain its being a *specific* fact. Whoever tells us then to search the facts to find the truth in general should also tell us what sorts of facts, what kinds of things, we are looking for. Where will we find the truth about men in general? In the facts of biology? Physics? Economics? History? Psychology? In all of them?—and put together, how? We have to have a general idea of what men are before we can make a search or survey of specific facts. General ideas give us the sense which has finally to be found in the facts themselves. It is not, of course, that we first have general ideas and only then go to the specific facts. But neither is it the other way around. We always have both the general and the specific, and we sort them out and adjust them to one another. Each gives a kind of meaning to the other; each would be empty or chaotic were it pure and by itself. It will not do, then, to wait for the truth in general, as if it would only at the last appear and then be altogether clear. To see the sense in the very facts we already know and to search out still further facts, we have no alternative but to set out and to criticize the general ideas we already have about man.

Now, the second theme: the intent in urging that human nature is seamless is good, but the idea itself is not finally true. We are in some way certainly the same. Only, we should understand our single human nature so that we make sense of the differences between us too. Neglect the differences and we think of our natures as buried and ineffective, as if they had no bearing on the distinctive ways in which we feel and think and act. Were we the same within, we should be the same without, and then we could not explain why we behave so differently. Not all the differences between us are superficial. There are different things we are fitted best to do; we have different values, paces, moods and sensitivities. To be understood, these have to be referred to our natures. Our natures cannot be so withdrawn and still that they do not shape and show themselves in the different sorts of things we do.

The major reasons for not venturing to think about kinds of men are, therefore, not so very strong. The caution of the first is too cautious; it prohibits thought entirely. The well-meant urgency of the second is too timid and narrow. We need wider and stronger notions that will explain the differences between us but still show that no kind of man is more valuable than the rest. The venture of this essay is to sketch out such ideas.

Its initial thesis is that we are not self-contained beings, but that, essentially, we interact with other sorts of things. They partly constitute us, or our activity. To explore our nature philosophically we have therefore to isolate the basic features of reality and to consider how we have to interact with them. The pivotal argument of the essay is that there are four fundamental realities and that these open up for us four distinctive ways of life. The basic realities are Individuals, the Good, Time and God. Our activity—no matter how narrowly directed it is—deals with all of them, with all of them together. Each of the realities, looked at carefully, is seen to provide both an access to the others and a way of connecting them together. When we act, then, we deal with the whole of things in one or another of four distinctive ways— either practically, through the agency of Individuals; rationally, through the Good; artistically, through the entry into everything which Time provides; or religiously, by reaching toward or acting on behalf of God. Some of us are thereby practical men; others of us are men of reason; some of us live our lives in art; and still others of us are religious. The different ways of life— Practice, Reason, Art and Religion—are the four faces of man. Each of them is endlessly demanding, and each is equally valuable and fulfilling.

These ideas—about dealing with everything in different ways— show that we have a common human nature but that we are also different kinds of men. Here and there, the sketch in this essay of the kinds of men will, of course, neglect details, and there is no question of fixing all the issues perfectly. Still, the claims are as forthright as I can make them. They will be:

1. Each man is essentially bound up with every other sort of thing; his concern is cosmic in range.
2. Though the range of concern is the same in all men, each of us channels or focuses the concern; we could not otherwise be both whole and individual.
3. There are four ways of focusing concern because there are four basic realities, each of which gives us an access to the others and also unifies them. The realities are Individuals, the Good, Time, and God.
4. Each of us is therefore either a practical man, a man of reason, a man of art, or a religious man. Our concern with everything is ordered through one of the four realities, in one of four different ways.
5. We do not deliberately choose our focus, though we have some choice about how we will show what kinds of men we are.
6. We may be unsure about what kind of men we are and never indeed find out. Those who are confident that they know their natures have usually been made sure of them in the crises which make their own values clear.
7. It is a mistake to think that everyone is the same in kind, the same as us, for example, only less or more excellent. The mistake leads to our making extravagant and inappropriate concessions and demands on other kinds of men.
8. Each of the four kinds of men exhibits traits which the others also have, but each orders them differently; a trait may be regent in one kind of man, subordinate in another.
9. There are no more than four kinds of men, and where the kinds appear to be mixed, one focus of concern is really dominant. There is no renaissance man, for example, and the philosopher-king, the king-priest, or the artist-philosopher is one or the other first, not both equally at once.
10. The four kinds of men are equal in value or importance. Practice, reason, art and religion are equally effective, discerning, appreciative and devout but none of them is fully adequate to the whole of things.

Each of these claims is supported in the chapters of this essay, sometimes by arguments about the ways in which we take account of different kinds of things, sometimes by illustrations which are aimed to induce their acceptability. The essay is neither a complete nor a thorough argument. Still, I think there is evidence enough in its sketches of the four kinds of men to warrant our thinking that its ten main claims are true. At the close, these reasons will be set out separately and finally reviewed.

In forming the ideas which are discussed here, I have been affected by the reflections of very many men, mainly philosophers, but then I have also tried to understand from practical men and artists and from religious men what they are concerned to do. Among the philosophers, my deepest debts are to Peirce, Aristotle, Descartes, Kant, and to the provocative thought of Paul Weiss, who was once a teacher and colleague of mine and who is now, in fine fullness, a dear friend. Other friends, John Burkett, Charles Day, Andrew Reck, Richard Sewall, Paul Tatter, Shirley Ward, Melvin Woody and Susan Woody have been generous enough to read and criticize my manuscript, and Florence Haywood has carefully prepared it for the Press. I am also in debt to Martha Lieb, my wife. Though she has all along insisted that neither she nor I nor anyone is only one of the four kinds of men I have described, she has with gracious patience borne my austere argument that she did not really understand.

I dedicate this book to the memory of my father, Moses Lewis Lieb. He was a practical man who feared God, loved song and story, and who wanted his children to understand the world.

Austin, Texas
1968

Chapter I

The Scope of Concern

———

We know a great deal about ourselves. We know, for example, how the cells or particles which are the very smallest parts of us are like the parts of other things. We understand something of our psyches too, of the deep urgencies we feel and the saving or subversive ingenuities through which they are expressed. We know about our societies, their forces and many aims. We know about language, art and piety, about wanting, making and using things; we understand the importance of being serious and having fun, and we have looked deeply into the meanings in suffering and death. We have enormous amounts of information about ourselves. Some of it is reliable and secure; some of it is only likely to be true. What we do not know is how this detailed information goes together, how so many sorts of things can all be true of us. We do not have a good general understanding of what men are. Not even the leading sciences help us much with that.

The reason they do not help is that no one of them tells us how its findings can be combined with those of the other sciences. The official, modest claim of each is that it studies this or that, not everything. One will study man as a physiological or chemical or physical system; another will look at us as a field of psychic forces. There are also studies of us as economic beings, historical creatures, and as creations of a special evolutionary or social destiny. We are studied as this or that, with each science seeing us in its special way.

Still, the sciences are not neatly compartmentalized. Even now, they jostle one another and there are immodest, unofficial claims. Physics, for example, crowds psychology. In effect it says that psychology will not much longer seem to be a separate science; what it covers badly now will soon be dealt with physically. Chemistry is suspicious of a separate science of biology; it is skeptical about the distinctive meanings found in history and sociology— as if there were not room enough for these sciences to be in their own terms true. The immodest claims are that one or another science is really basic and that its results are the proper basis for other studies which, by comparison, are more specialized. Were there to be a single science, one which studies everything, it would of course deal with us as well, without fragmenting us. We have no such science now. Should we wait for one? Are there prospects of our ever having one?

There seem not to be. Although several sciences claim for themselves the key and basic place, the question of which of them is really first is not a scientific one. No science can claim that it studies all there is to know. The generic natures of the things a science studies, how far a science can ever go—these questions can be settled, but no science can settle them. No science now, none that there could ever be, can explain the large ideas we need for explaining everything. Each is partial, and it has to be. The world is too varied in its specific stuffs and forms to be comprehended in a single formula. The principles of a science need to be sharply definite—so definite that no science can contain all we want to know. None can even tell us all we want to know about man in general. We have to learn from the sciences, of course. But we have to venture along a different route as well.

The route of this essay is speculative and philosophical. It starts from what we know and proceeds from there, feeling for the sense that must be found in things. It is critical and imaginative—responsive to the obscurities that occur when we aim to know only of specific things. It also tries to preserve specific knowledge and to adjust it in an informed but wider view. Speculative philosophy is a variety of knowing, and not an unfamiliar one. Many of us engage in it. Its route is the one we need as we refine our ideas about the nature of man in general.

The simplest speculative philosophy—many think it is the safest one—is simply to combine some of the results of the sciences: it is to draw a picture of us based on the sciences, to claim that we are composites, conglomerates of parts which are the separate subjects of scientific inquiry. No single science tells us about man in general; each studies only a part of us. But since the parts are in fact all conjoined in us, were we imaginatively to combine the results of the sciences, perhaps we would see what we are—we are complicated assemblies of parts, powers or agencies.

This idea is very popular. It has been developed many times and, naturally, there have been many claims about the catalogue, the number and the kinds, of parts. Usually, the inventories include a body, a mind and a will or some other urgent drive or appetite or sensitivity. Biology, chemistry, psychology, history or sociology—imaginatively combined—these should tell us what we are. The idea is that a man is a body, a mind, a will or appetite, that we are all of these at once. Together, parts like these make up an individual man.

The trouble with this idea is that it cannot tell us how our parts combine. We are not, we do not feel ourselves to be, a packed array of bits and pieces, piled or glued. The idea has no place for the very *we* who decides whether we are a conglomerate or not. It also fails to see that parts which are not parts of a single thing are not really parts at all.

But should we not say something like this, though? Is not something like this right?—not perhaps that we are a parcel of separate parts but rather that we are a web or net of powers or active agencies, a field in which several distinctive forces play? Many think that this sort of view is sound. Will it really do?

The answer, I think, is "no, not finally," for two serious difficulties in this idea cannot be set aside. First, powers that cooperate

3

or oppose one another can be neither entirely separate nor distinctive—so it cannot be right to say that we are a field of separate energies. Then too, and more important, the view has no way of explaining how it is that we are singular or individual. Who is the *I* in which the distinctive forces play? Am I too a power, one among the others? Or am I something else, not a power, but something which nevertheless powerfully constrains the powers which are inside of me? Neither suggestion, and these are the large options, enables us to understand the idea that we are a web of agencies. The difficulties are important. Let me review them in more detail.

First, about the separateness and distinctiveness of the powers: think, for instance, of a body which is thought to work together with a mind and will. Such a body cannot be wholly "bodily," for it understands what a separate mind thinks that it should do. It must therefore have a diminutive mind of its own. It must also have its own urgencies which a separate will exploits or overcomes. It is a body with bodily wisdom and appetite, not very different from a so-called separate mind and will, and such loss of distinctness also occurs with other of our agencies. A mind that works with other parts of us has to be something like a bodily force and a directed will, and the same is true of a will that works with other of our agencies.

Powers that cooperate or even war with one another, then, have to be more versatile than they were first thought to be; they have to be very like the powers they oppose or join, and they cannot be sharply distinguished from them. Together, the powers are supposed to explain what it is for us to be a man, but each of them turns out to be a separate "little man," and then, uselessly, since the "little men" have themselves to be understood, they too have to be divided into parts: the diminutive mind of a body, for example, should be distinguished from the body which has the mind. Distinctions such as these, however, can be made regressively, without an end. There is therefore no level on which our so-called separate powers are separate, and an explanation or understanding which supposes that they are separate will either never start or end. It is therefore unacceptable.

Even if the notion of our having separate powers were somehow understandable, the question would still remain of just what or who we are. What is it for a man to have a power or for him to have his powers issue out from him? Were a man himself a power, he would be only one among *his* other powers; he could hardly be said to have *them*. The unity, the center, the singleness we think that a man has could not be accounted for. We would see a man as a medley of powers but not as a singular individual.

Suppose, though, to try still another time, that a man is not a power but is instead a kind of field or border, a form or limit within which his powers are found. He could then be said to *have* the powers he constrains, and there are still other advantages to such a view. For instance, it allows for a man's location; we can even think of something as being inside and outside of him. Still, in spite of this advantage, we need to see a man as more than a located being. He also acts, and no conception of him will be sound if it does not allow for his activity. Unfortunately, notions of a border or a limit picture him in rigid inactivity. Were he to be a border for the powers within him, he would do nothing except keep them in; he would be a restraining surface for them. From time to time, perhaps, he would be moved about by his own vitality, but even then *he* would be doing nothing himself, not even changing. The notion, then, that a man is some sort of boundary for his powers construes him mistakenly. It does not let us see that man can move and change, and grow and act; nor does it help even with the important notion of self-control. It is too limited to be a sound conception of man and his activity.

No matter how we turn the idea that we are a congeries of distinctive powers, we come to strains in it which make it unacceptable. The claim that our powers are distinct seems to be unsound, and the question of who we are, if we are not a power, is answered either obscurely or mistakenly. The view of man we hoped to find in using the idea of separate powers does not show us the details we need to see. We need some new ideas. We should no longer try to claim that we are a conglomerate of separate parts or even powers. If parts of us are separate, they are not really parts and there is no conglomerate of them. If we are single beings, there are no separate agencies inside us.

Still, the idea that there are parts of us or that there are different powers in us is very hard to set aside. We will see later what truth there is in it, and perhaps, in patience for the idea, one more version of it should be considered even now: the idea that we are indeed made up of parts or forces, but that these do not coexist in a nice democracy; there is a monarchy or tyranny among our parts—one part of us is regent and the others are subservient to it. The subservient parts may be surly, and now and then unresponsive. At death, they will each go their own way, but while we are alive, there is a ruler, and other parts of us are ruled by him.

Who, on such a view, is the monarch? We are, of course; but then what are we? Some have supposed that we are minds, that a man *is* a mind and that he *has* a body and other parts. He *has* them; they are parts of him and he rules them more or less. Or, there are other views: for instance, that we *are* bodies who *have* minds or wills, or that we *are* wills which surge through bodies and are channeled through minds but which dominate them, so that the separate aims of minds and bodies are subordinate to a ruling will. There are still other candidates for the regency. One regent, though, is all such theory will allow. It is because there is only one that we are single beings, and it is by our dominion over other powers that our complexity, our inner conflicts and our supple effectiveness are all explained. Regency, out of fashion elsewhere, still seems to many of us the right view of our own nature. Is this the sort of view we ought to hold?

Again, the answer, I think, is "no," because the most crucial notions in this view cannot be explained. One thing is said to *have* another; a regency is exercised upon the other parts of us. But the *having* and the *ruling* cannot be understood. No part of us can be wise, devious or powerful enough to rule what other separate parts of us shall do.

Suppose, for example, that a mind were the regent. The mind is said to have a body because it can control what the body does. But how can it do that? It is not a body itself; it cannot push the body around. How then does it exercise its regency? Is it by thinking what its body ought to do? Thinking, though, the sort of thinking that a regent mind can do, will not restrain a body. To control its body through its thought, the mind would have to set its thought before the body and have the body accept the thought as its own aim. But the body either has an aim of its own or not. If it has one of its own, it would have to be forced or persuaded to forsake its aim and undertake a new one. If it has none, it would have to be given one. Without bodily force, however, a mind cannot force an aim upon a body, and if a mind were to persuade or allure or deceive a body, the body, once again, could not be merely bodily. It would have a mind of its own, one to which suggestions could be submitted and in which resolution could be shaped. We would then have a mind, and a body with a mind, and then, as we saw before, we would still have to understand how the mind which is in the body forces or persuades its body into doing anything. The regent will have a chancellor who will have a sub-chancellor who will have a sub-chancellor, and there will be no subjects after all.

The controls are no more feasible if we think of a body or of a will or indeed of anything else as regent. If we are conglomerates of different things or powers, no one of them can rule on all the rest. Their distinctiveness, their separateness, render them incapable of rule. If we want to think of ourselves as complex but still as single entities, we will have to understand our complexity so that our parts are really parts of us. For this understanding, though, we will have to see ourselves differently, not as pieced together with parts which are studied in the special sciences, nor even indeed as an assemblage of separate powers. Would it be better, then, to see ourselves as a single, supple power dealing in different ways with different things? Instead of thinking that we combine or are a combination of powers, would it be better to think that we are a single power, so adroit that we can seem even to turn against ourselves? This is perhaps the most widespread of contemporary views.

THE VITAL PRINCIPLE

We can do many sorts of things. Is there a single power by which our acts are brought about? It is plausible to think there is. For if we had more than one power, we could not see ourselves as the same in all our acts. We could not even see our acts as ours. If we are individuals addressed outward from ourselves, if we are the same, no matter what we do, the only explanation for both our sameness and singularity, or so it seems, is a single power which animates us all the time. It is quickened sometimes in high intensity; at other times it is quiescent; there are times when it is almost uncontrolled; finally, it diminishes and life fades. This, then, is the view: we are the same in all our acts because there is one power in them; our acts are ours, for all of their variety, because they are produced by a single source of our vitality.

Supposing there were a single power in each of us, how should it be described? There have been many suggestions. Our power is sometimes said to be the power of life; sometimes, eros or yearning or will; sometimes it is said to be reason, sexuality, creativity or concern. There are a dozen words for it. Some stress its assertiveness; some, its aims; some mark its distinctive access to the world.

Regardless of the name, the idea is that there is a single pool or source or kind of energy. It seeps or flows or surges through us, vitalizing us. It makes for the doing in our every act. It explains even the doing of different sorts of acts. It is ubiquitous, expressed now through mind, now through body, now through both at once. It is not suppressible. It always finds some exit for itself. When things outside us, for example, resist one expression of it, it finds another for itself, or it makes us find it one. Or, if one part of ourselves has blocked its way, our power comes out through another channel. Suppressed, it is never stilled. We cannot restrain but only shape its course. The expressions which we allow it or which it makes for itself may not be fulfilling ones, but then, perhaps, that is what explains its endless restlessness.

This is an enormously revealing view. Many people are persuaded by it, and some of the facts of science seem to support it too. There are separate entities, separate centers of activity. Something moves them in their activity. Only a power can do that, and if the activity in things is their own activity, if they are the doers, then the power in their activity must be in them. There cannot, therefore, be a single overriding cosmic power. If there were, there would be no individuals who act. Still, while there are individual acts, individuals are active at the same time and together; they interact in a common world. Their powers are separate, then, but they are also congenial or commensurate; the powers are alike. Every active thing has a power of the same kind. The differences in the way in which the power is used, the different acts that result from this power, must be explained by referring to something in the acting entities themselves—perhaps the amount of power they have, or the control they have on it, or the bodies through which the power is shown. All that needs to be explained can be explained, or so it at first appears.

There are, however, anomalies in this view, and there are things that are too unclear. Ironically, what is most unclear is the main idea itself, the idea that we are a power or that we have a power and that we make use of it. What is it to have a power or to be a power, and to have that power be expressed? How shall we understand (1) that we have within us the vital stuff of our next activity, that the force which makes for our future acts is within us now? How shall we understand (2) that our power is not demonic, that it does not possess us, and (3) that we can control it without having still another power, different from the one which we control? Then too, how are we to explain (4) that, whether we will or not, our power and the power of other things courses out in measured, lawlike pace, and (5) that our power can do what it is supposed to do, vitalize a body and cause an act? These questions bring out the anomalies. The answers to them are strained and implausible. Both the questions and the answers suggest where the idea of "power" is not clear enough to help us see who we are and what it is for us to act.

The cause of the unclarity is a mistaken basic view of us. We think of ourselves as having a single power because we first think of ourselves in a certain way. Then, building on that picture of ourselves, the view that we elaborate is patched together to cover the mistake; here and there, as a consequence, it becomes opaque. Unclearness in a view always marks a mistake in it; it is not an obscuring covering upon a thought. What, then is the basic picture which leads us to think that we have a single power? What is the mistake in it? How, saving the plausibility in the picture, can the mistake be set aside?

The mistake is to think that we are at each moment stopped, that there is a now, a sheer moment, and that we are located at that moment and have then to move on from it. The mistake is to think of us as located at an instant in which we do not act, and of our then starting in to act. With what? If we are stationary, if a moment is stopped or we are stopped in the moment, we can act only if we possess something which, while stilled in that moment too, is able to move or push us or permit us to vitalize ourselves. This is exactly what a power is supposed to do. The word "power" stands for a stuff which is a part of us while we are stopped and which also enables us to move. Possessed in a stilled moment, a power is quiescent; we can do something but we are not doing it just then. Nevertheless, with a power or because of it, we can start to act. It is as our power issues or surges into us that we change or move.

The idea that we have a single power answers this question for us: *how shall we think of ourselves as capable of activity when, after all, we are merely here and in an instant now?* The answer is that we possess something which, while also here and now, can vitalize us and be the cause of our activity. Given the question, the answer is unavoidable. We need not be bound to the answer, however, for the question is itself miscast. It is a mistake to think that we are located in a stilled moment, and the idea of power which grows out of this mistake should be set aside. What is plausible in the notion has to be reshaped. The idea of "power" should be formed anew, just as the question it is used to answer has to be reformed.

The reason this mistake has not been widely seen is simply that we have made it hard to see. We think of ourselves as being located in an instant, but then we also think of the instants as run together. This makes the stillness of the moments almost undetectable. It even seems to show that we are active all the time. Then, since it is true that we are always active, and since a power is supposed to move us in our activity, this notion of a power looks perfectly all right; it seems to be an essential part of the soundest view of us. It seems this way, however, only when we overlook the connection between an idea of power and an idea of stilled moments. This is the oversight we bring to notice when we ask ourselves just what it is for us to act. Then we see that a notion of power which is fitted to an idea of moments of inactivity cannot give us the understanding we need. Instants, run together, remain stilled, and therefore an idea of power which goes with stilled moments cannot explain what it is supposed to make most clear—how a power can vitalize us in or through or after the moment in which we are still. Running moments together only obscures the issues. When we see them, we see that our question about action was not well formed and that, at the start, faulty notions had to be made up and called into use.

The idea that a single power moves us is a fiction constructed to fill in a picture of us which we have no reason to think is true. Many reasons can in fact show the picture to be wrong. Set the picture aside, or correct it, and more appropriate notions come into view. What are these notions? How do they help us to see ourselves and our activity? There is no understanding what a power is or how it can move us if ever we are stilled. But, then, what picture should replace this important view?

THE CONTEXT OF MAN

The most useful way to find the notions we need is to redraw the part of the picture which leads us so astray, and then to amend the rest of it. Instead of saying that we are stilled in a moment or that the moment we are in is stilled, we should see that each moment is a passage and that we are active in it too. This is to be our starting claim. We are ever-active beings, and action, as we will see, is always interaction. We act on and together with others and other sorts of things. We also act because of them and as opposed to them. We should think of ourselves, then, as always active, never stilled, and we should see what other sorts of things contribute to our activity. These, the basic kinds of things, are the context for our activity. To understand ourselves we have to refer to them as well.

Perhaps the first lines in the picture we are to draw should be about the time in our activity. If we are always active, no moment is ever stopped in us. In every moment, however, there is passage and activity both for time and for ourselves, not for one of these alone. Time does not surge over us, with us unmoving, firm and steady, set against its tide. Nor is it that only we are active, as if we moved against a background of eternity and time's passing were itself unreal. There is at every moment change for time and a change for ourselves, and these changes interlace: time passes in part because of us and we are changed in part by it.

Active, never stopped or still, we are nevertheless not identical with the acts which we perform. We engage in acts; we are in our acts; but we are not the same as them. We are, therefore, not sheer streams of transience, tissue thin; the whole of us is not in the nowness of what is now. Those who claim that we have buried powers and potentialities are right to see that there is more to us than is found in any present time. Mistakenly, however, they suppose that the passing of time is basic, that the passing is intrinsic to time and not at all owed to anything else. For them, our powers have to be buried under the passing which goes on overhead. But the anomaly in this is that the buried powers have still to keep up with the time-tossed body they are thought to vitalize; they have, after all, to move along in passing time. We should avoid this anomaly but still stay with the view that we are not wholly in a present time. The best way to do this—though it is unusual—is to claim that the passage of time is not a basic fact. We are to see that, while real, passage is itself derived, that it comes about because of other things—among them, things like us, firm enough to make a change of time. For all our activity, then, we should not see ourselves as sheafs of change, as Whitehead recommends. We are things to which and in which change occurs, and, in turn, we change other sorts of things. One of the things we interact with is time itself. In our picture of ourselves, then, we have to think of an entity which we can label "time." Its nature is quite different from our own.

Changes that affect time are, for most of us, the hardest ones to understand. This is because we are accustomed to thinking of time as the most embracing of realities: everything changes inside of it while it is unchanged by what it holds. A number of theologians and philosophers have, however, shown us how to modify this view. They point out and argue that some realities are not held within a passing time; there are realities partly aside from passage, and they affect it some. We need, perhaps, not go so far or in the same direction as these philosophers and theologians do, to talk, for example, of creation, providence or destiny. It will be enough if we can see that we and other things stand somewhat apart from time, and that we act so as to provoke it into yielding new futurities and to cause its passing to occur.

Our claim, then, is that passage itself comes about—though of course time does not take time to pass. Its passing is an interplay of different sorts of things. Unfamiliar as this idea is to us, it has been seen for a long while in the East. There, thinkers have often claimed that time's passing is unreal; passing, they think, is an appearance of something still more basic or more real. Their view is that what is finally real is a single, timeless sort of thing. There seems, however, to be a contradiction in this claim, for were there a single, homogeneous reality, nothing could appear. Passage could not be illusory; it would not have even that minimal reality. When we correct this mistake by holding that there are, not just one, but several basic sorts of things, we can agree with the Eastern thinkers that time's passage is derived, but then, unlike them, we will also think of it as a necessary interplay of things and not in the least unreal.

How, though, should this interplay be understood? A present moment comes about, or the presentness of what is in it comes about because time interacts with other things. This is what is claimed. But is it true? What is the passage in which the present comes to be? How and why does time yield itself into a moment of present time?

Time comes to pass because individuals are active. Individuals, however, act on and toward and with, not only time, but other realities as well. These other realities therefore have to be considered in explaining the interplay between time and individuals. In the past, indeed, the great answers that were given to questions about time's passage appealed to them even more than to individuals. For example, reference has often been made to a demiurge, or to a pure or perfect thing, or even to God—to something which forces or urges time into presentness; or to something which provides the conditions under which time surges naturally into certain enduring forms. It is as if in those answers two sorts of realities were being isolated: (1) a demiurge or God, something active but not transient, and (2) the forms or species or modes of definiteness which order or shape what passes in time or the passage of time itself. These two sorts of realities have, of course, been said to be connected, and we will find that an appeal to them, or to entities like them is unavoidable. They will have to be in our picture too, but they do not have a prominent role in explaining the fact that time issues into us at a present. Individuals are prominent in the constitution of this fact. Time is not lured or forced into being present. Nor is there a present time because time is the medium for God's eternally creative aim. Both these themes in the answers of the past suppose that a non-temporal activity causes the passage in a present time. They seem to be only partly right. It is better, even if unusual, to say that time becomes present to keep itself whole and singular, to save itself from the jeopardy which individuals cause for it, which we and things like us cause for it. The jeopardy occurs as each of us takes time into ourselves. We are temporal beings; we have an age and we become older. We subordinate time in ourselves and thereby try to sheer off from it a portion for ourselves. To keep itself whole and singular, time therefore rushes onto us and into us. It is common to and for us all. But as each of us separately incorporates it in himself, time moves on, wresting from us what we have wrest from it, preserving itself as singular by being, now, a past. Time divides into present, past and future because of us, because we provoke it to the change it has to make to be a single entity. Its dumb necessity is in its ever doing what causes it the very jeopardy which provokes its change—moving on to us. Through our provocation of it, we affect it some. It also changes us in turn.

Some of the changes which time causes in us occur as time helps us to be and remain contemporaries of other individuals. We are not each separately set into time; it is not a coincidence that many of us are located at a present time. But, then, we are contemporaries of one another not merely in being at the same present moment, but in being active now as well. Time binds us together not only as items at a moment but also as active beings. It presents itself in us both as we are contemporaries of one another, and also as we are changing beings, versatile enough to last awhile through passing time.

And what is it for an individual to last? It is not having a solid, inner core which is untouched by passing surface play. It is an achievement; it takes activity, and activity is also interactivity; it is done in connection with something else. Our lasting has in fact to be an interplay with some singular entity which is not caught up in transience in the way we are ourselves. We interact with time, but we have to interact with another reality to last through passing time. This reality has to be something like a god, something whose being is not jeopardized in passage. It has to be something which is not a *mere* contemporary of ours, something to which each of us can appeal to explain how, interacting with it, we can stay the same but last as long, or less or longer, than our several contemporaries. Our lasting cannot solely be an interacting with things that come and go. We could not be or be recognized as self-same throughout a time were that to be the case. A singular god is the only being that can be the constant correlate of singular and changing things, and god's constancy in connection with us helps to explain how individuals, singly, and as together with other individuals, last self-same through a period of time. A god, then, too, has to be a part of the context in which we live.

Buddhists, as we know, take a different view of our lasting and of our being connected with a singular god. They tell us to leave transience aside, to escape from it. They think that we can escape, and that we seem to ourselves singular only as long as we dally in the transient. As we let it go, they think that true reality is revealed, and that there are no individuals, no single beings, no tasks, no aims; there is no singular god apart from us. All limited singularities are, for Buddhists, a mistake. But what if they are not? If we are individual right now, if there is no escape for us from transience, if as individuals we last, then the only explanation for these facts will have to be that there is a singular being which is not a contemporary of ours, which is not jeopardized in transience, but which nevertheless enters in some way into our activities. We have no alternative but to claim these *ifs* as fact. The consequence is that, while being together with other individuals, we are the same moment to moment, not merely or solely in our own right, but in connection with a being which does not face the same risks as we. Time, then, has not only to present itself so as to provide for our being contemporary with other individuals; its wholeness has also to allow for a connection between individuals and a reality which is, unlike ourselves, not bound inescapably in passing time. It cannot do these things by being the moving image of eternity. Even as it is a whole, time must have movement inside of it.

We too, in our own way, change inside ourselves. We last while we are changing, and were we not to change we could not last. There is no passing of time except as there are changes within it, changes of some sort. Why is it that we have to change? The answer is simply that we cannot be still; we could not be at all if we were still. We are forced to activity because of the actions of other things, by our contemporaries, for example, or by time's threat to make us wholly past. We cannot help but change. What we should especially note about our changes, though, is that while they occur now and then, the changes occur inside the single encompassing activity in which we are engaged throughout our lives. This will seem a strange idea, of course, if we think that there are no generic activities, if we think of ourselves as engaged now in one activity and now in another, so that we complete one and then stand at rest until a fresh urgency impels us to act anew. It is true indeed that we engage in specific activities. But these are ours only as they are portions of a single activity in which we are always engaged, now at different paces, now with different focused aims. Our activity has to be seen somehow as a single whole; we could not otherwise understand ourselves as being the singular centers of all we do. Our activities are parts of a single task; they are the specific ways, the different ways, in which we do some single thing. This single, general activity is what we mean by living, or by the having of a life.

Now, the next and last step is to ask how it is that we can have a single activity, a life, an extended one? How is it that time issues into it? What explains the fact of there being generic activity? It too has to rest on an interaction. Is there some single thing at which we always aim, something so distant that it can provide for the extensiveness of life? Some of the classical Greek thinkers are supposed to have believed that this was so—that there is a Good toward which we are always striving, which is good because we are finally aimed at it and which is, because of being good, the measure of all other and foreshortened aims. Is this sound or not? Something like the Good has, I think, finally to be supposed, but not in quite the way in which the Greeks first thought of it. One change, at least, has to be made in the notion, and we have also to see that the Good is not the only reality which can explain how our lives are a single activity.

The change is simply to construe the Good so that it is not the measure or test of the value of everything, or not the only measure of things. The Good, as the Greeks held, is always exhibited; it is not a distant, future thing. But it may be exhibited well or not, and if that is true, the Good cannot be the measure of everything. It cannot measure the good of its being shown and of its being shown as it is. It can only measure things for the Good they show, and the value of the Good itself, and of its being exhibited, has to be measured by appeal to something else. Nothing is the measure of its own value, and everything, even when it is valuable for what is in itself, has to have its value measured by some other thing. It seems, then, that if we are to claim that there is something like a platonic Good, we cannot cast it as the measure of all values. Like God and time and individuals, the Good is a measure of value. But its distinctive importance for men is in providing for the intelligibility and generality of our activity.

Do we really need such a notion as the Good? It may seem more ideal, less real, than the other realities that have been mentioned. It may seem that the Good is only a word and there is nothing real for which it stands. These, however, are, I think, only the appearances of the Good. To see its reality, we have to look into things for the way in which the Good in them becomes emphatic for our thought. It has this emphasis as we see, when things are together, that they have a character which makes them intelligible and thereby comparable to other things, at any time and anywhere. This character, the character which makes for comparability, is not theirs as wholly then and there. It is the Good in them. Let me now try to be clearer about this character.

The contemporary world, for example, can be compared to the world of the Romans and the Greeks; it can also be compared to a world which might still be made. For there to be such comparison, there must be some character which is exhibited whenever things are together, and that character cannot wholly derive (1) from time or the individuals which are in time, or even (2) from a god. (1) Individuals in time are contemporaries, but their own contribution to their being contemporaries is simply to be a medley of things opposed to one another in space. Neither they nor time, then, can be the source of a trait which is exhibited at any time and by *every* thing. (2) Nor can this strand in things be owed, let us say, to God. Many thinkers identify the Good and God. In this essay, the two are distinguished, and they are distinguished because distinct features of our activity can, it seems, be explained only by supposing that we interact with different sorts of things. In connection with ourselves, God answers to our privacies; it is to him that we look to explain the fact of our lasting and being self-same. To explain that we and our activity incorporate a general and intelligible and partly public character we have to appeal to something else. Grant a difference between intelligible publicity and privileged privacy and no alternative remains but to hold that the generic character which makes for the intelligibility and comparability in individuals is owed to our interplay with a reality different from time and God. It is this reality (to use an old and established name) which will here be called the Good.

The Good, then, is what makes for the sense which things have as being together and which also makes for each one of them being understandable. Since there are meanings and comparisons that we can see, since we can see how things stand, thus escaping the idiosyncrasy of our own specific place among them, there must be a strand in things which is always exhibited. This feature in individuals is not owed to the individuals alone, or to time, or to God, though they are also involved in its exhibition. It must therefore be owed to something real in its own right. We sense this trait in individuals when we are not dominated by the bruteness of the here and now, not blinded by fleeting shifts of transience, or not absorbed in deep responsiveness to God. Philosophers and others whose main concern is to know and understand have, of all men, been best able to make out the configurations of this character. This is because the Good is most prominent in their concern. The Good, however, is not, as many philosophers have thought, the most basic feature of the real. It is but one among others, interleaved with features which men of other dispositions have seen with equal surety.

While not the measure of all values, the Good has to be acknowledged as both basic and real. It is the character which we discern in understanding an individual, and it provides the context in which we understand how things stand to all the other things with which they are joined. Time does not suffuse it, except as it is exhibited in the things in which time is shown as transience. Not exhausted in its exhibitions, the Good nevertheless can and must ever be exhibited. It, thereby, defines time as a futurity for things, and it stabilizes time by its own singleness, lending to it a measured regularity. The Good, like God and time and individuals, is part structure and part substance in all there is. It is not the end at which, inescapably, all of us must aim. Each basic reality can have this role. To be active beings we must have some end to which we have ever to adjust. This end may be the Good or not. In either case, the Good is always a portion in all our activity.

Some of these last remarks, many of them perhaps, will not seem clear enough. Then too, the parts which are clear may not seem right. Perhaps, though, the claims will seem more definite and cogent as we go along, later parts throwing light on those which have been set out first. What has been set out so far are the main lines of a sketch of our place among all the things there are. The sketch shows that we are ever-active beings, caught up with others in a contemporary world, though the transience which marks the world does not reach us through and through. It is, in fact, to us and to other things like us that the transience in the world is owed. Time suffuses us continually because both it and we are bounded by and addressed to still further realities. To explain this bounding and connectedness, we must suppose that there is a being, not itself caught in transience, toward whom we are addressed, and it is our connection with this being which explains the fact that we can be the same even while we change. We can think of it as God, or as a kind of god. Finally, there is another reality which has also to be taken into account. To use an old name again, it is called the Good. The Good is exhibited in all that occurs, and it explains the intelligible continuity we find in things. All these sorts of things, then—individuals, time, God and the Good—combine together to make the whole of things. They combine in different ways, and each makes a distinctive contribution to the totality. No one of them binds up all the rest. We are ourselves addressed to everything, to the others who are our contemporaries, to time, to God and to the Good. We do not face a single reality alone; no one sort of thing defines our human kind. We are addressed to the totality of things. But because each kind of thing provides an access to all the rest, because each kind of thing in its own way unifies the rest, we can address ourselves to everything in different ways.

This last claim is the most distinctive feature of this picture of ourselves. In all the other pictures of us which I have read about, one sort of thing is claimed to be most real, most privileged, most demanding, most revealing—so that in these other pictures we are seen as dealing with everything by aiming at it through the one most real sort of thing, through the state, for example, or through knowledge, or through God and proper piety. But if there are different sorts of things, if none of them is more basic, more revelatory than the rest, if each of them provides a way of unifying all the others, then we may deal with everything in different ways, and no single way can claim to be pre-eminent. Our picture, then, is a picture of us as addressed outward, dealing with everything, with every sort of reality. This is our continuous and singular activity. But our picture also shows that there are different sorts of things, each of which contributes in its own way to the totality it makes with all the rest. Each, then, provides for us an access to the others, so that we can deal with them in different but equal ways. This is the picture which has now to be filled in. The fact that we take account of different strands in things will then show the root sense in the idea that there are parts in us; and the idea of a single aim will reshape acceptably the notion that we are a single power or that we have a power which we use. First, though, less abstractly, something more should be said about our addressing everything, about the nature which is ours as men.

MAN'S NATURE

What is distinctive about us? What marks us off from other things, from even those which we resemble most? There are a dozen answers to these questions. We are animals, or we are very like them. Almost all the answers begin this way. But then we are rational animals, or language-using or symbol-making animals, and it is perhaps because of this that we are also the only animals who really laugh and cry. Or, we are religious beings, lower than the angels but kin to what is lower still. We are the only beings who can and need to pray. Or, perhaps our distinctiveness is that we are moral animals; our every act is either right or wrong. Or, as has also been said many times, we are the only animals who engage in art and games, or the only ones who are political, not merely social, and the only ones who work.

None of these accounts is wrong; each accents an important or special feature of us. But each slogan has narrow partisans who think that it provides the basic truth about us, and that the other slogans are true only as consequences of the more basic truth they claim. Take, for example, a partisan claim on behalf of rationality. Granted, rationality is fragile; that has always been known. But if rationality is our most distinctive mark, then it explains everything else which is essentially true of us. To be rational is to be able to apprehend the *ratio* in things, to understand them and to acknowledge what others can acknowledge too. We thereby escape the binding idiosyncrasies of narrow privacies, and it is no surprise that, between men, there should then be talk about what we understand and what we can and ought to do. Art and play, in turn, are preparations for a more demanding rationality; they are forms of rationality, designed for relief and for the young in whom rationality has not yet come to prominence. A partisan for rationality will find something like this to be true even for religion, and he would urge that our politics are or should be rationally incorporated in stabilized practices which contribute to the development of thought. Taking rationality as the most basic of our distinctive features, one can claim that all our activities are rational, in one guise or another, in greater or in less degree.

This same claim to priority, however, can be made equally for the other slogans. Think of men as specially created by God, and it is easy to think that thought and speech are special gifts which are confounded when they are misused but which, when rightly used, help us toward proper piety. Art, demanding practicalities, politics, these too have their advocates, those who claim that they are the ways in which most distinctively we address the whole of things. But, now, what are we to make of these competing claims? Which of them should we advocate? We will find our way here only if we understand why there are competing claims, why it is that one or another claim is said to be the right perspective on our activities. The answers to these questions have already been suggested and partly argued for.

There are competing claims because their advocates have different views about what kinds of things there are and how these things combine. The advocate of a basic rationality supposes that all our dealings with things are filtered through our thoughts. Everything, to him, every sort of thing, is dealt with through understanding it, and understanding things is seeing them as special cases of a lucid, overarching principle. Every activity is, therefore, rational; more rational as instances of the principle are clear in being instances of it, less so as they are smeared and streaked with sensuosities, so that it is unsettled just what they are. The basis for the claim about the priority of rationality is simply that a principle which is acknowledged by reason both unifies everything real and provides for our access to it. Everything is an instance or a condition or a qualification upon the instances of the basic reality through which we understand. That is why reason is first in us and all else is subordinate.

But this same sort of justification, as should now be clear, is also provided by those who claim that we are fundamentally not rational, but something else. Instead of saying that everything is an instance of an overriding principle of rationality, something else can be claimed as being in the basic place; something else accounts for such unity as things together have. He who sees us as essentially religious sees everything as created or sustained by God, so that, for him, the only way we can deal with everything is in accord with God's governance of it. He thinks that we always have to account to God and that we can do this with more or less fidelity. Then too, there have been arguments to show that neither reason nor God accounts for the togetherness of all things, that something else does this in another way, and that we have no option but to deal with things through such access to them as their favored first principle provides. The competing claims are claims about how different sorts of things are together, and they compete because each holds that we have to deal with everything in but a single way, through the entry to it which their preferred first entity provides.

Which of these claims should we advocate? Which of them is most likely to be sound? Our distinctiveness is surely shown in our activity, and it may seem, therefore, that there can be only one way in which, basically, we deal with things, that there can be only one reality which embraces or creates or sustains or controls whatever else is real. We have, therefore, only to isolate that singular reality and make our claim on behalf of it.

This easy course, however, is not open to us because no one of the exclusive and excluding claims is altogether true. The only reason there could be for making any one of the claims has already been ruled out. The preceding section, which set out a new picture of ourselves, argued that no one reality provides exclusive access to all the rest. The argument was that there are four basic realities, that these are partly independent of one another and partly not, and that each, in its own way, unifies the rest. No one sort of thing, it was said, envelops all the others while, imperious, it has no need for them. Every basic sort of thing has some bearing on the rest; each provides us with a way of dealing with them all. The bearing on everything through individuals is called "practice." Dealing with everything through the access to it which the Good provides is "reason." Art encompasses all reality through the reality of time, and religion embraces everything through God. There are, then, many ways of dealing with the whole of things, not just one, and no one way is best or better than the rest. Since there are good reasons for thinking there is more than one access to the whole of things, and good reasons too for believing that no one access is more fully adequate than another, we cannot make a claim to define ourselves exclusively or even best by reason or religion, by art or even politics. No one of these special claims tells us wholly who we are. We will describe ourselves far better by urging that all the claims are true, or rather, that each of us is one or another of the kinds of men that these claims describe, but that no one of the claims properly declares the natures of all the human kind.

As men, we are all concerned for the whole of things in the distinctively human way; we are all alike, our natures are the same. The divisions of reality, the basic kinds of things—individuals, the Good, time and God—enable us to be clearer about our natures. We can say what we are in general and we can also say, specifically, what kinds of men we are.

In general, we are concerned to deal with the whole of things through the access to them which one strand of reality provides. We try to bring everything together in one or another of the four different ways in which things can be brought together. We can be said to act on behalf of a basic reality, to represent it in our dealings with the world. We are thereby representative beings, while other animals and things, it seems, are not.

Specifically, we are of different kinds depending on the strand of reality through which we deal with the other realities and toward which we aim. Dealing with everything through one strand of things defines our ends specifically. Shall it be our end to promote justice or the general welfare? Shall it be our end to have the Good made pervasive of the whole of things, to do God's will, or to have harmonies override whatever disproportions cannot be removed from the world? Perhaps—depending on the kinds of men we are. No end in itself (could there be such a thing?) can be either definite or binding upon us all.

As humans, then, we have a common nature, and it is shown in our concern to deal with everything through one strand of reality. The kinds of men we are, the kinds of lives we have, depend on the routes we take in acting in the world. These routes, and the texture of our lives as we develop them, have now more fully to be explored. Each kind of life, as we will see, shows in its own way that we are concerned with everything.

Chapter II

The World of Practice

_____

Who is the man of practice? What is he concerned to do? Like all of us, he is concerned for everything, only his concern is practical; it is focused in a certain way. He deals with everything as a center of agency. Each is to be confronted or avoided, overcome or submitted to; each is to be used as a means or made into a confederate. In practice, a man is occupied with agencies, with his own and with the agencies of other individuals, and he acts to do what needs to be done now and next and after that.

The most insistent needs of the man of practice are those that sustain, promote and extend his agency. Threatening individuals are to be confronted; food and shelter have to be secured; cities and states must be made to run. The first intent of the practical man is with the near and close at hand, with what is pressing now. Beyond that, however, other threats are always in the offing. A practical man may postpone dealing with them, hoping that they will not intensify or that others will work with them on his behalf. But he may also try to treat the near at hand so as effectively to settle on tomorrow too. Here and there it has become possible for a man of practice to look to present threats and promises in ways that are so indirect they do not seem practical at all. No matter, though, how far removed from the solid ground of goings-on his way with things may seem, it is in the stubborn resistances and insistences from day to day that a man of practice is finally occupied.

Men of practice may seem, of course, to take delight in what does not seem practical at all. They may enjoy themselves in art and sports, for example, or spend spare time in study and reflection; they may derive deep satisfactions from their church. They are often generous and serious about what does not bear at once on practical affairs. But for all the energy they invest in them, these interests always stand somewhat to the side, and even then these interests bear on practicalities: renewing and refreshing practical men, leading to strategies and plans, helping to steady perseverance. The center, the focus of concern, for men of practice is with the bearing that events have for continuing agency, with what happens through a course of passing time. They try to deal with things mightily.

Because of the might they have, men of practice often seem to be of gigantic proportion, and they find it useful to be seen as larger than real size. They are the subjects of public notice, powerful, threatening or benign. We all talk about them, and it is difficult for men who are not practical to avoid being tempted and intimidated by men who have got and can use such notoriety. In centuries past, these large-sized men were pictured as caesar, soldier-king, knight and merchant prince. Nowadays, the images are of the masterful statesman, the executive and the general. In normal scale, there are many varieties of practical people: farmers, craftsmen, workmen, salesmen, housewives. For each of them, the world is a world of things that threaten his agency or promise to enlarge it; it is a place in which, from day to day, the continuing insistences of active things must be dealt with so that he can survive.

To deal with the world in practice, to make sure of what he needs to have, the man of practice tries to fix and to control what he finds about him now. He tries to preserve and protect it, and to see that he will have the same or more control in the future. Everyone who has ever reflected on practice has noted that in practice we tend to press beyond the borders of the place in which we have control. If we control what is within our province, dangers can come only from outside. The spreading wildness of the woods threatens the farmer; the warriors of the next country threaten the king. The capitalist claims that the Communists are intent on world domination; in turn, the Communists say that capitalists want unrestrained control. The language of each is extravagent; each, nevertheless, has a cause for fear.

Insisting on what is needed, securing it—these are essential to the man of practice. He may try to secure it alone or in community, but whatever his means, he has always to be alert to the boundaries of his domain. Since there always are, beyond whatever place he then controls, new threats for him to meet, in practice he is driven singly or with others to seek dominion over everything. Since the world changes from day to day in the going on of time, he tries in practice to make his mastery last, and to preserve the place he has won. No one can himself endure through all of passing time, but then, a man of practice tries to pass his mastery on, in crafts and methods, in the institutions in which he invests his life, in families, in businesses and, to use the most affectionately strident of practical terms, in the father or the mother land.

Men of practice, then, like other men, aim to deal with everything. They aim to deal with it practically, and to be practical is to wrest the agency from things, to make them part of ourselves or part of our own agency, or it is to subdue them, or make them docile and subservient, to avoid them or to join with them in a kind of community. No sort of thing stands beyond the reach of this concern. We can deal practically with each other, with time, with both God and the Good, though never, as we will see, with full success.

Because practice is varied and demanding, practical men must be thoughtful too. This need, however, does not make them men of reason. They neither want nor need to know the natures of things. They have to know *how* to deal with them. The two are different. Practical problems are not intellectual problems; and practical action is not a muscular supplement to prior thought, as if knowing *what* something is were the same or could lead at once or readily to knowing *how* to deal with it. We can know what something is before we act on it. But knowing how to make use of it is always a part of practical activity. It is in the activity itself. It is not a staid or settled knowing but is adjusted constantly to control the changes which occur in action and which could not have been foreseen. For example, understanding the theory of flight is different from knowing how to fly a plane. Each flight is different, not just an instance of the theory we already understand. All of a plane's motions and changes have then and there knowingly to be controlled. The thoughtfulness of a man of practice is in knowing *how,* not the "useless" knowing that this is *what* things are. He comes to this sort of knowing in practice, through practicing, not through theory, not even through a theory about the way theories are applied.

Still, men of practice do not leave aside the perspective through which men of reason try to treat the whole of things. They simply use it practically. Where men of reason understand that this or that is actually the case by confirming what they knew first as possible, practical men take what they actually encounter as token of what is possible; it is a signal of what can come about. The words "possible" and "actual" do not mean the same for both of them. For each of them, however, the same principle connects the separate meanings they have for these two terms. Men of reason see things through the principle. They go from the possible through a principle to understanding what actually occurs. Men of practice find the same principle to be a limiting and revealing trait encountered in all the things with which they have to deal. They take account of it, so to speak, from its underside. They have a kind of knowledge, then, but they are not men of reason because of that. Their knowledge is distinctly practical.

Then too, practical men are attentive to what most concerns artists and religious men. As practical, however, they are neither artistic nor religious, though this does not mean that they are brutes without sensitivity or men without a final aim. Men who fail in practice, because of insensitivity or lack of devotion in their aim, fail in being practical, not because they are not men of a different kind. Practice has ample room for the traits which other sorts of men make central to their lives. In practice, however, their role and shape is practical.

No strand of reality is left aside by practice. We do not have the question of muse or merchandise, of God or the profane. Practice, in its way, will have them both, as in their own ways art and religion also do. Practice is like art in its incorporated skills and its productiveness; but the stage only represents the world, it is not the same as it. Then too, like religion, practice reaches through all of time and yields up its communities, only it forces us into public communion while our privacies are kept submerged. Religion, on the other hand, has our community derive from essentially private confessions, promoted, perhaps, and steadied and stabilized in a public world.

Practice neglects no feature of the world. It deals with what men of reason, art and faith are concerned to emphasize, but it deals with it in its own way, to achieve an end which it itself defines. It incorporates a kind of knowledge, artistry, even piety, practically. It is a distinct domain. We can best start to understand it by seeing first the force of the overstated claim that, of all enterprises, practice is primary, the most basic kind of life.

PRACTICE AS PRIMARY

Practical men often think of themselves as thick-skinned, unsentimental and hardheaded, robust enough to battle elements and to win what we need before all else, a place, safe for a time, against the hazards of the world. There are many theorists who also think of practice as basic. Their theory is that we have first to have food, shelter and clothing—these are necessities; only afterward can there be the luxuries of reflection, art and piety. We have to live before we can live well, and it is by practice that our basic livelihood is won. Everything else rests upon this base; and it is proper and appropriate only as it refines our basic practicality. When constructions are not aligned well with the base, they are unstable and we cannot live in them, at least as full-bodied men. We become effete, airy, vague and vagrant, no longer able to deal with the real world. We are said to be parasites upon the men who stay in touch with things. The remedy is to return to the fuller world, to go back to nature, to do some work. The earth, the sea, perhaps the sky, are said to restore us. For all its brutality, the primitive is sound. It is the basis for all soundness, and proper reason; art and faith stay close to it.

On the view which holds that practice is basic, everything is practical, more or less. Reason, art and faith are not impractical, or they need not be. They are simply not urgently practical; they emphasize features of reality in which there is little of the urgent thrust of agency. When there is a respite in our dealings with the world, or when some of us can be spared from the most direct confrontation with it, these, the gentler, features can be separately attended to. They can be isolated, contemplated, elaborated, even celebrated, so that, on this view, when we go from practice to less urgent enterprise, we do not move entirely away from it. We deal with but parts of the world in an attenuated practice, and though we are thereby less full as men, for the time at least, we can both afford and enjoy the partiality. Fullest practice, then, has no need to be critical of such less strenuous activity. From time to time one needs to ask only that it be lessened, or that it more directly support our basic activity. These are the appropriate practical demands.

Practice, on this view, has, however, always to be attentive for the perversions which might occur when we withdraw from thickest practicalities. Thought, art and religion can move from practice and then, aberrantly, seem to lose all touch with it. They may even turn against it, or so it seems, and then practice will override them, as we will see. Theorists of practice, alert to unsound departures, try to make clear just where and how far from practice thought and art and faith can go and still stay within reach of it. Their injunction is that practice is primary and that except as thought bears on practice, it is not thought at all, and that art and religion can also become vaporous.

Pragmatism is the most well developed theory about thought and the primacy of practice. It says that we think in order to establish beliefs and that explicit beliefs are resolutions about how we could or would act practically. All ideas, all meaningful ones, can occur as parts of beliefs, and the meaning of an idea is an idea of the possible effects which could be caused by the thing the idea is about. Thoughts have different meanings if they are about different, conceivable practical effects; they mean the same, no matter what their formulations, if they are not about different possible effects. What accompanies our thought but is not about conceivable effects is not itself a thought; it is a feeling or other sensation which only a confused man would take to be a thought. For the pragmatist, practice or possible practice is what occasions thought, and all meaningful ideas are about the possible ingredients of practice. Thought is aimed at practice; it is not done for its own sake, and possible and actual practice are the measures of its meaning and its truth.

There could be corresponding pragmatisms for art and religion. None, however, has been developed with thorough care. There have been programs, suggestions and injunctions but—to take art first—no full theory has yet described the portions of practice which art refines, nor has any explained the creativeness of art or its bearing on practicalities. Some theorists have held that art is the same as thought, only that in art our thought is decorated with attractive sensuosities. They can hold a standard pragmatic view and then caution us about the seductiveness of the decorative. Others, more discerning about the differences between art and thought, urge that art is not about anything at all. Its significance is not that it signifies but that it is important; it can shape and perfect our attitudes. It does not represent things or tell about them. It expresses what we feel and it promotes our having the feelings it conveys. The artist, according to this view, is a practical man. He is a craftsman who engenders, controls and aims the feelings he provokes. Since feelings, stabilized in attitudes, are important for what we do, there is a connecting line between art and basic practicalities. There have been still other suggestions about the connections between the two. The theme of all of them is the same: that art is attenuated practice and that, however indirect its way, its aim is to support the fullest of our worldly activity.

This same theme, stated with suitable tenderness, could also be found in a pragmatism for religion. There have been formulations of such a view (Mordecai Kaplan's claim that religion is really a civilization, for example) but here too ideas have not yet been set out comprehensively. Perhaps this is because old sentiments are against the formulations, but then, even so, the sentiments are effective only against the formulations, not against the development of religious pragmatisms in fact. There have recently been enormous changes in religious practice: in the councils, in service and liturgy, and especially in the pastorate. Pastors have ventured into labor, civil strife, issues of public policy, and war and peace. Their congregations have become those they have joined and formed and led. If religion seeks to serve us where we are, and not to draw us to itself, if we are wrapped in practice, it must come there too. There are many nowadays who feel this way. They care little whether their practice is called religious or secular; the name makes no difference practically. For them, religion has to risk the presumption that practice can lead us to see what God has willed as our destiny. The goods of practice are, therefore, to be the aim of religious men. Practice purified by practice shows us what is genuinely God's will, so that a basic practice can be thought to rule even on what is right religiously.

Make practice basic, see it as inescapable, and the other "sorts" of things we do will differ from it only in degree. They are less practical and more luxurious; they are not really needed for the having of a life. They do not define a full and different kind of life; they only qualify the life of practice by accenting a part of it. Basic practice fixes what they are and it rules on their propriety. It is the ground of the features which they emphasize; it provides their aim; it is therefore the authority for their conduct. This is what the primacy of practice means.

This claim of practice to primacy is harsh, overstated and finally unsound; perhaps it is not even practical. It is a revealing view of great power because it is partly right. It is right in seeing that everything has a bearing upon practice. Nothing is irrelevant to practice; nothing stands beyond its reach. It goes too far, however, in claiming that the whole being of things is their being in practice, that their meaning is wholly their meaning for practice, and that their only value is in supporting the aim of practical activity. While nothing stands entirely apart from practice, it is a mistake and a corruption of practice to claim that everything is exclusively inside of it.

How is this to be shown? How is the overstatement to be hedged in? The briefest way, perhaps, will be to consider what so-called basic practice is supposed to be. This will not deny that there is practice or that practice is a distinctive way of acting, of dealing with the world. But it will enable us to see that what is not practical is not therefore only a modification or refinement of practical activity.

Take eating, for example. We are told that eating is a necessity, that it is needed before we can engage in less practical activities, and of course everyone has to eat. But what is basic eating, what is the kind of eating which it is necessary for us to do? If there were such an eating, it would not be a part of a distinctive kind of life; it would be only a preliminary to such a life. No activity, however, stands first, before a kind of life. There is therefore no activity of merely eating, or merely anything else. The word "eating" is not the name of a definite activity which is basically practical, and only then, with one or another of its features stressed, that same practicality refined. There are differences between feeding, nurturing, nourishing and sustaining ourselves. Some have distinguished between foods for the body, mind, imagination and spirit. These and other distinctions about what, when, where, why and with whom we are to eat testify to there being no unqualified eating which is so basic and practical that all other eating is a variant of it. We do not first eat and only then have our distinctive aims. Eating is an activity in an aimed life, and it thereby always has a distinctive form, perhaps practical, perhaps not. There is practical eating, just as there is practical knowing. But it is one kind of eating, no more basic than the other kinds. The same is true for clothing and shelter, for all the so-called basic practicalities.

The idea that there is some basic practicality on which all else is built is a practical idea, an effective one. But it is also an overstated idea. For when we try to isolate practice as basic, in providing food, clothing, or shelter, for example, we find nothing definite enough to be a base for all else. Nothing stands apart from or before our having a kind of life. What is definitely practical is on the same level with, not more basic than, our other ways of dealing with the world.

To hedge the overstatement, then, to limit it to proper bounds, we should say that while everything can be dealt with in practice, practice is not the only way to take full hold on things. It can deal with everything in its own way, but it is not the only way to deal with them. Ironically, if we don't feel for the partiality and limit of practice, we are likely to have our own practice fail. Practice is difficult, in any case. As with other ways of dealing with the world, it never succeeds entirely. It can have distinctive successes and failures. These are what we have now to explore. We have seen practice as standing alongside other enterprises. Now we have to see it by itself. This will show us better what practice is and allow us to ask about its proprieties and the goods which it makes available.

A GENERAL THEORY OF ACTIVITY

There is a blind spot in our understanding of action. We know what it means to intend to act. We can also look back on an action and say what it was and whether it was done well or not. Forward and backward visions are clear. Action itself, however, is blurred. What is opaque in action is the occurring, the happening, the pushing and pressuring as something is being done. It is as if, in prospect, things stand still enough for us to make out what they are, and that they are also still, their configuration fixed, once action is all through, but that in activity itself, in the interval between future and past, things are too unsettled to be known. Even descriptions of action are indirect; our talk of it always mentions the future or the past: what is happening is what we planned or hoped or feared, or it is like what has happened in the past. We know the *what* of an action, but only before or afterward, not in the action itself. There, it seems, the *what* is being formed. It may or may not be what we envisioned or what we had seen before. We simply cannot tell until it is stable and all there.

Our not being able to see the *what* of an ongoing action is not a defect in knowledge. In fact, it shows us what is most distinctive about this sort of knowing and about how it gets at things. To know *what* something is we have to isolate the thing and see it as an instance of something else. We can have this kind of knowing, then, only when there is an instance or the prospect of having one. When an instance is in the making, there is nothing yet to know; there is no thing which is this or that; no *what* is complete in the going on. This is true even if we claim that knowing something is the same as knowing what it does. We have still to have an *it* to know, and to have the doing either in a prospect or all done. A doing, a causing, a producing, as it is going on, has no *what* in it that we can know. A *what* is known only beforehand or afterward.

Even though there is no definite *what* in an activity for us to penetrate, there is much about activities which we can always understand. We can see, for example, why there have to be activities, what sorts of things enter into them, and why and how a *what* occurs. Activity itself may be a blur to intellect, but its rationale can be made out. We only have to put the issues properly, and the start, in doing this, is to see again that we, that all individuals, are always active, and that our activities are interactivities. We interact both with other individuals and with other sorts of things. Starting from these claims—they were argued earlier—in this section I will try to show (1) in general, that in our actions we interplay with each and with all of the kinds of reality—with individuals, the Good, time and God: the interplay constitutes our activity; and (2) in particular, I will also try to show that action is of a kind depending on which of these basic realities provides the entry to the others and the unity which we are concerned to provide for all of them. Practical action, as we will see, is the kind of action which is specifically aimed at everything through our own agency and the agency of other individuals.

Let me begin with evident and prominent features of our activity. Perhaps the most prominent accent in our activity is that there are other things in it besides ourselves. We act on them, with them, toward them, for or against them. In our activity, other individuals and different kinds of things are made to come together in a slightly different way than they were before. Our distinctness from the things we act on is the mark in us that we are things which act. In particular, our imposing on other individuals and resisting them, having and seeking a place from which they are excluded, is what defines us as an individual. Lose the difference and opposition, and activity, its very possibility, is gone. Imposition and resistance, however, are not characters in an instant. There has to be passage for them to occur. Individuals have to impose on one another and resist the imposition. Yet, for all the opposition, individuals and other realities are joined together in activity. The rationale of activity is in seeing how the individuals and other realities join together in the making of a course of time.

We and the things with which we interact are always being made to present ourselves to one another. We are forced or pushed or carried into fresh presentness, whether we want to be or not. There is more to us than our being in any present. We have an inside, as it were, as well as a surface; it is the something of us which is not merely here and now. Were we to be surface only, we would have neither past nor future. We would not interact with anything, nor could we provoke the passage in which we are swept along. Our surfaces, then, are boundaries, but not for ourselves alone. What forces us to the surface and into a new presentness is time itself. It moves responsively to the jeopardy we make by appropriating it, but it is not only at the surface that we are joined with time. That portion or mode of our own being which is not presented to another now, our inside, is itself caught up with the time which will be in transience; it is not independent of time, so that something new of us and a new present moment occur together by coincidence. There is no coincidence in this at all. That in us which has not been presented to others yet will also come to presentness.

The idea that our inside, our unpresented being, is tissued through with time is an idea of potentiality, somewhat like Aristotle's great idea. The comparison, the difference on this important point, may help to make the idea clear: where Aristotle thinks that our potentiality issues into a present because we are ever drawn to imitate the activity of a completed actuality, the idea here is that we are carried into presentness by a time with which we are intertwined and which we provoke to transience. This idea connects time and us more closely than Aristotle's does; though in agreement with Aristotle, it also says that the mere issuing of ourselves into a present is not yet an action on our part. For action, we have not only to enter or be made to enter in a present, we have to be presented to other things and to interact with them as well. Together now with other individuals, coerced as they also are into a new presentness, our interaction with them has still to be understood. It is an action in which we are made and may make ourselves more definite. Aristotle again, provides a suggestion about the nature of this activity.

He thinks that the things about us shape the ways in which our potentiality is shown. An acorn has, he says, a distinctive potentiality; it cannot become just anything, but whether it becomes an oak or not depends partly on other substances. They are responsible for the accidental features in the development of the acorn; they enter into its activity. How do they do that? The answer seems to be that as a potentiality issues out, it is strained by a form but not entirely restrained by it. There is more to potentiality, there is more of it and more urgency in it, than a form is able to constrain. The unrestrained, only partly shaped potentiality exudes outward from the thing. It fouls the definiteness which is owed to the form and is intrusive on other things. These, in their stability, resist the effusive potentiality and thereby shape it from outside. Because it is already partly shaped by "its own" form, the renegade potency is only partly congenial to other forms. At its edges, then, a substance is jointly shaped by its own form and by surrounding things or by the forms they have. In turn, of course, the outside shapers have potencies of their own, and they also need help in shaping their own coursing urgencies. By nature, there is a mutual aid arrangement: one thing helps to limit the potencies of others; in turn, they limit its excessiveness. Things do for one another what they are unable finally to do for themselves.

This view of Aristotle's is very penetrating; it helps us to understand a great deal. There seem, however, to be some serious flaws in it. For one, what others do in the final shaping of our potencies is not merely done to us, it is done for us as well, and we have to appropriate the definiteness of the features which they cause us to have. Our borders are fixed by others, but we must make them our own. There is unfortunately nothing in Aristotle's view which explains how this is done. A form which channels potency cannot reach out to claim what it did not restrain. How then are we to understand that we are single beings when others fix what becomes a part of us? An Aristotelian form is perhaps not inert, but we need a notion of something more versatile in us than such a form could ever be.

Then too, the effects on us of other things have to be more enduring and more effective than Aristotle sees. We would not develop otherwise. Were a form only a channel for our potency, were it unable to change itself or be altered by what occurs, we never would mature. In each moment, we would be shaped in the same way, and we would be bordered by momentary accidents. What there is in us which is owed to other things would be gone without a trace; it would not modify the form of our regular activity. Since, for Aristotle, things outside us seem to qualify only what our form is not able to direct, the form itself, for him, cannot be affected by such change. We therefore cannot change, nor can we have our natures changed, and this view is a mistake. The mistake charged here is a version of the old complaint that Aristotle could not see that forms evolve. It is a strong version, for it explains not only why the forms are never changed but also why, if we think of form as Aristotle does, we cannot even say how anything develops to maturity. What happens to us must be seen as part of us, and it must also make a difference to us later on. Aristotle's ideas of form and potency should be modified to allow for that.

The first change should be to claim that while each individual has potentiality, its potency is not singular, not a private pool of power, not a potency separate from the potencies of other individuals. Our potencies are not distinct, nor are we sharply singular in that portion of our being which is not exhibited in oppositions here and now. Our future is merged with the future of other individuals; we ourselves are merged with them so far as there is more to us than our being in a present time. It is a mistake to think of potentialities as parceled out, one each to a separate individual. Even Aristotle seemed unable consistently to go this far, for on his view, a potentiality is definite or can be known only if uniform behavior by other things is also presupposed.

It would, however, be a mistake to go too far the other way, to claim as some philosophers have done, that since our being is merged with others such individuality as we have is not quite real or that, finally, there are no separate individuals. We are singular and especially definite as here and now, but we are also merged with others and with the time which we provoke into a passing presentness. Aristotle is mainly right about our present interactiveness. Buddhists, on the other hand—they hold the polar view—are right about our not having individuality in nontransient time. To hold with both at once, we should see that potentialities are not private possessions but are an issuing into our imposing and resisting individualities of that being of ours which is merged with other individuals. With this as the first change in Aristotle's view, the second is quite plain.

Because our potentiality is not a private pool of force, we can not think of ourselves merely as shapers of the force which irrepressibly surges out of us. We are not simply stolid things which have a form. We are active, through and through and, as opposed to Aristotle, our view should be that even our persistence is an activity. We persist as we create something of our persisting selves anew, and when we cannot make this creative addition, we no longer last. Persisting, then, is not a matter of being stolid or, somehow, stolidly having a form. It is appropriating for ourselves some of the being which is carried onto us in an inrushing temporality. We do not claim this being as a right and have it portioned out to us. We seize it by ourselves, for ourselves; we lay hold of it, and we do this through that of ourselves which resists the time which carries something of us into an ineffective past. There are irremedial losses of our being at every moment, but the whole of us is not in each moment lost. Without our doing anything, then, oncoming temporality is partly channelized by the resistance we offer it and partly by time's portioning itself in the attempt to redeem the separate appropriations we have already made of it. Still, we are active too. What we do is retain something of ourselves in the present and, through it, we seize hold of our own being in an oncoming time. What we then take hold of becomes more definite as our being in a present time, and what is retained in us into a present is made to supervene upon the newly definite. Persisting—seizing for ourselves and unifying in us the being we share with others—is an activity or part of an activity of ours. It is, however, not the only thing we do. Indeed, it is qualified by three other actions or features of activity. Our action is a conjunct of the four.

(1) In a present, as we persist, we also present ourselves to other individuals. They are our contemporaries and we interact with them. Partly, this interaction is owed to time. It rushes over us,

and we careen into one another as we take hold of the being time brings within our reach. We can overpower one another, make others subordinate their activity to ours, or even cause them not to last. Your futurity and mine are not neatly portioned out. How I take hold of the being we have each to individualize affects what you will be, and the other way around of course as well. While acting to persist, then, we also interact. This interaction is part of our public side and it is more or less controlled.

We can shape the seizures we will make of the being which comes within our grasp. Because we are limited, however, we cannot lay hold on all of it; we cannot become the only individual or even ruler of all the rest. Our retained pasts are too limited for that, and our versatility is too small. We would tear ourselves apart in trying to capture and hold on to all that will issue into the course of time, which is perhaps part of what should be meant by the saying about power's corrupting us. Still, restrained though they are, our seizures affect every other individual; we infect others with ourselves. We are spread out and forced against them, but, again, we do not dominate them all. Besides the limitation of our power, we are also limited by the fact that as we appropriate time and oppose other individuals, we also address both God and the Good. Connection with them is a part of our activity.

(2) Our spread outward, our push and press against the things around us now, is the outside of our activity. There is, as it were, an inner aspect too. The partly channeled time which rushes over us has to be drawn in; our borders have to be made more firm. Action, while aimed outward, also has an inward strain. It has its vital rhythm; it goes out but also in. The outward strain is, as we have seen, an interaction, but the inward is interactive too. It is not an insulated change, enclosed "inside" an individual. It is a move toward something else, an adjustment on our part. It is a move with respect to God and it is made even if we are not or not much aware of it or not especially concerned because of it. We "relocate" ourselves in action with respect to the things around us and to time. We also locate ourselves in connection with God. He provides for one dimension of our activity.

We can move inward, laying hold of our own surface and of passing time because we are creatures of more than a moment. Something of the non-present in our being has already been brought out in the discussions of our potency, of that being of ours which is merged with the being of other individuals. But there are also other strands in our being which are non-present. Were potency the only one, we could not explain our lasting and certain other features of our activity. One other strand in our non-present being has to do with God. Indeed our very moving inward to appropriate our surface and our presentness is owed to that in us through which we stand in connection with God. This connection, then, is a nontransient dimension of our activity. Action is not through and through temporal in the same sense of "temporality." We all see this, even in saying something as familiar as that in acting we change, that we move from here to there, get older, and behave well or badly in what we do. There are layers of temporality, different senses of "temporality" in an action; or rather, an action is a juncture of our dealings with different sorts of things. Our move inward is not merely a move away from the transience which spreads through our surfaces. It is, as it were, a move in connection with God.

If we were not connected with God we would not be persistent individuals. We would be momentary events, all surface, all transient, not individuals or not able to act at all. Were we somehow individual for a moment but apart from God, we could not retain our individuality. Our potencies do not individuate us; nor does our spread against others mark off our borders well. It is only as we appropriate the overrunning transience that we are individual. Time or space or matter do not individuate us. We individuate ourselves by using them, and we cannot do this except as we move with respect to God. Without him, transience would seep through us without limit or restraint. We could not last or perhaps, in any sense, be individual. Our connectedness with God is the ground for our persistent individuality.

As we are connected with God, he sustains us. He does not cause us to exist, though it is a small mistake to think he does, a confusion of "sustaining" and "existing." Existing has to do with opposition and interaction, fighting for a place. Sustaining has to do with a nonpassing connection between God and ourselves. We would of course not exist unless we were also sustained, but this means only that our existence is indirectly owed to God; our will and power are our own. The name which has been most often used for the activity in which we are sustained is "love." It stands for a union in which two joined things remain two, patient, neither one forcing itself nor intruding on the other, but such that because of the love, the loved ones may deal with everything else in a loving way. One who sees how God's sustaining us can bear upon our dealings with other things may say that God fills us with light, with the light which permits us to see how things really are; or he will talk about God's being wise. The light or wisdom have to do with God's bearing on other things through and because of us. The love, the sustaining, however, is primary, even if we are not attentive to it and do little for or because of God.

One mode of our action, then, is found in our connection with God. This is the dimension to which religious men are most attentive, and they would like to have it prominent in all activity. It occurs, prominent or not, in all activity, even in the activity in which practice is our main concern, as we will see. It has to be there, for we could not otherwise understand our being either persistent or individual. Action is not an event, an occurrence; it has depth. Nor is it an issuing out of ourselves, as if we constrained our powers and then released them against other things. Were this last the case, there would be no commonality of time, and the rhythms of nature would show nothing of our own caste. With a time that overruns us all, with our having to appropriate it and individualize ourselves still more, there must be in us a move toward something neither passing nor potential. A move toward God is an inescapable aspect or direction in all our activity. The final dimension of our activity is in connection with the Good.

(3) The outward and inward strains of action tend to pull us apart. We may go one way more than another; we may be "this worldly" or not. We cannot, however, be so caught in the tissues of transience that we have no recessive privacy, nor can we retreat so far that we leave all worldly things aside. Public men have private lives; saints and meditative men have to master their bodies or bear them as being burdensome. The stretch between inward and outward, this continuity in ourselves, is where our joining with the Good is made most evident. This overlap is often called our nature, and its continuity between inner and outer often makes both us and the nature seem to be ambiguous, as if we were all essence or all accident, as if we were not individuals at all or

had no natures in our individuality. The soundest view, I think, is to hold the extremes of both these ambiguities, to see us and others as always specializing afresh the Good which we incorporate. Our natures will then be principles of action, permanent, yet specified in the course of time. We can hold this if we see again that, while being individual, we are not entirely definite or self-enclosed.

Whether individuals are definite or not has been a point of torment in philosophy. Many thinkers have tried to settle the "ambiguity" decisively, one way or the other—either by claiming that the definiteness of character which occurs in the world is not owed to individuals at all, so that there are really no "separate" individuals or only momentary ones; or the "ambiguity" is settled by claiming that individuals are entirely determinate, that they either incorporate essential natures or are so radically definite that they are sheer existents, with no generality at all. Plato, for example, can be seen as holding to a view of the first sort: for him, there are no individuals which, while apart from the Good, act to incorporate the Good within themselves. The Good itself provides for whatever intelligible features come to be within the world; apart from the Good nothing is definite enough to be, or to be called, an individual. Aristotle and Leibniz, on the other hand, take the second view: there are, for them, individuals, and the individuals have forms or natures on their own. Some existentialists should be seen, perhaps, as taking an extreme version of this view— that individuals are so individual that there is in them no basis even for comparing individuals. Both of these opposing views seem to me too extreme as an explanation of individuality. Too much in our natures and in our actions are, according to them, unexplainable. It would be better, I think, to go between the extremes, to bear the "ambiguity," and to hold that rather than being intolerable, the "ambiguity" says what is in fact true: that we are partly definite and partly not; in particular that while we are not entirely definite and while we need others to make us more so, on our own we are always steady enough and aimed enough to incorporate the Good.

The Good as specialized in us is the distinctiveness in our appropriating overriding transience so as to stand both together with and distinct from the other things which are around us now. We press out against these other things; we appropriate passing temporality; we move inward to stand before God; we specialize the Good—we do all these things, so to speak, at once. We could not do one of them without doing the others. There is therefore no question of doing the others first and turning to the Good only at the last. The Good is always specialized in us; we do not decide whether to specialize it or not, though we have some control on its issue into us. To specialize the Good is not to grab a part of it and pull it into us. The Good is not divisible, we cannot make it or part of it private in ourselves. Instead, it is focused in us as the way in which we stand to God and time and to other individuals. Its definiteness for us and in us is not owed to there already being definite species of the Good at which we aim or which God or some other being makes especially available. This last is Whitehead's view—correct in holding that the Good which occurs in us specifically does depend on how we stand to God, but mistaken, it seems, in claiming that it depends wholly on God's special selectivity. How we specialize the Good affects our connection with God just as much as the other way around. It is the same with time and other individuals. How we stand to them affects the Good's being specified in us; how we focus the Good bears on our connectedness to them.

How definite the Good becomes for us, then, depends on how lucid are our connections with others and other sorts of things; these dealings in turn affect our focus on the Good. A man who acts on a clear principle is unambiguously located in the world; the Good is very definite in him and it is plain how he stands to other of the strands of reality. In others of us, the case is perhaps not so plain. In either case, we specialize the Good by fixing how we will stand to the other realities. We may have little choice in this if they bear on us very heavily. But because the Good is specialized, it is always affected some by us, and there is always some room for us to shape our own intent.

Then too, because it is the whole Good and not a part of it which is specialized in us, because our hold on it is conditioned by our dealings with other things, some of which will specialize it too, the Good is a principle of order and uniformity within the world. It is what makes for regularity, though not in the finality of each detail. There is always some vagueness in the join between the Good and individuals. Individuals, and other kinds of things as well, seem sometimes to divide the Good. The Good, however, is singular; it must therefore always provide an order for individuals and an order in them as well. Neither the world nor any individual has ever been or will ever be completely chaotic.

These last reflections about the modes or strands of our activity are, I know, extremely abstract. The points they set out, however, should help us to understand what, concretely, an action is. Except as we see that there are layers or several dimensions in an action, except as we see that actions are made up of connections which are very like to whole actions themselves, we will not understand what they are. One who claims that in an action "things" are moved about by force, for example, sees at best only one feature of an activity. If this feature is all he sees, he will not understand that some individuals are born and grow or even that he himself has found out about the forces which push things from place to place. Likewise, one who thinks about what are called activities of mind, about knowing or planning or worrying, will make small sense even of these if he neglects the dimensions of activity to which we appeal to account for our bodies and our lasting in the world. Most of our talk about action is partial and limited. There is nothing wrong in this, if we acknowledge the partiality and see something of the fuller reality. It is that fuller reality, with its dimensions and different temporalities, which is sketched out here. The sketch is of activity in general—the activity in which individuals press out against one another, appropriate their present temporality, stand to God and specialize the Good.

If there were not these dimensions in activity, if activity were not a conjunct of these four adjustments, we could not account for species of activity and for our ambiguities about what kinds of actions are being done. The energetic wife says that her intellectual husband is doing nothing; he says that he is thinking and that thinking is an important job. A man in public life tries to do some private good; his critics find out about it and charge that he behaved politically. A painter produces a work of art; others say that painting is a waste of time. There would be no excuse for different readings of action if there were not different strands in all we do. It is in fact because of the strands that the several readings each make a kind of sense. That is also why every action can be read as practical, more or less, or as rational, or as a piece of artistry, or as sacred or profane. We cannot claim that an action is all four of these kinds. But we should not neglect its complexity. We have to preserve our sense for the several dimensions of an action even when we think of it as being of a distinctive kind. The way to mark out a kind of activity is not to deny its complexity but to note which of its dimensions is most prominent and unifying. We can see how this is done by turning now, specifically, to practical activity.

Practical action—at the center of our attention in this chapter—is activity in which our concern for everything is focused through our pressing on and standing firm against other individuals. If the demands of practice are imperative, the subordinate strands in our activity will not affect the action much. There will have to be some effect, however. How much there is depends on how able we are (1) in attending through practice to our connectedness with God, the Good and time and (2) in making adjustments to God, the Good, and time while we withstand the press of other individuals and direct our aim. This double role of a mode of being marks a species of activity.

The double role can be accented by using the familiar notions of means and ends. They are not entirely accurate here, but then neither are they altogether inappropriate. The accent is simply that action is of a kind, it divides into kinds, as a basic reality is (1) a means as well as (2) an end.

(1) In the case of practice, we are concerned to maintain ourselves along with and against the things that are around us now. By being with them, resisting and opposing them, we also then and there deal with everything else. The individuals about us are, as it were, a *means* for dealing with other realities.

The inaccuracy here is that our end in practice is not to deal with God, the Good and time by means of the individuals. We nevertheless affect these realities because of the qualifications they introduce in the things we are focused on. So far as you are touched by God, the Good and time, my press upon you qualifies them too. Hegel, Marx and the pragmatists seem to have been right in claiming that my every action is cosmic in its range, even if not mightily effective.

(2) On the other hand, I can be attentive to God, the Good and time and try to take such account of them as will support my

standing with and against other individuals. They are, as it were, *means* to the end of my being with these individuals. I may even sometimes suppose that they are magically effective or that I can make them so: that God can intercede in practice to preserve me from a threat, that nature in its regularity will not practically allow so terrible an occurrence, that even time will at my behest be stopped.

The inaccuracy here is that if practice is an end, God, the Good and time are never means to our achieving it; they are not practical means. The notions of means and ends are therefore not entirely appropriate for describing the distinctive mark of a kind of activity. They only suggest what has to be set out in longer terms: the distinctive mark of a kind of action is the two-ply character of a single kind of being. Centered upon one basic reality, other kinds of things are affected in what we do; and if we are attentive to them, we can perhaps deal still more effectively with the reality at which we aim—going, in practical action, through other individuals to deal with everything else and taking account of those other things to enhance our dealing with individuals. Such a double role for a reality, as we will see, also defines rational, artistic and religious activity.

The fact that the practical action of individuals reaches into all kinds of things and that it is qualified by them should soften some of the harshness in the judgments that practice is at root brutal, coercive, based on might alone. These judgments are appropriate, for practice is basically might, oppression and resistance—it is basically so, even when it is gentled by theory, skill and piety. The condemning intent of the judgments, however, is not finally sound. There can be great joys and goods in opposition and resistance. There can be horrors in them too, as there can be in an aim focused toward any basic reality. Men have lived in aching terror before God, in wretched, hurting ignorance in trying to deal with the Good, and in repellent ugliness in their struggle to capture the tenors of time. Every kind of action has its fulfillments and failures. Practice and the might that it incorporates, basic as a kind of activity, has a right which is not derived from any other sort of thing. The old question whether might as such is right is therefore badly phrased because there is no might unqualified. In practice, might is qualified by every sort of thing, and every sort of thing is dealt with mightily. The only question is whether in action we are able to deal mightily enough with every sort of thing, or whether, as happens to each of us at last, our might, however qualified, is not enough to make us full as individuals.

There are difficulties to practice that intellectual, artistic and religious men only rarely appreciate or understand. They are not intellectual difficulties, or artistic or religious ones. They have to do with might, with the opposing and resisting that are the basic notes of practice. They are sometimes so difficult that practical men feel constrained to coerce other sorts of men into helping them. We should now consider what these difficulties are and how, if we are not practical enough, we will not merely misunderstand but also misuse the other sorts of men.

THE COURSE AND GOOD OF PRACTICE

No one has ever sorted out the varieties of practice, not even for the earliest or simplest of our communities. A number of schemes describe primitive situations and suggest how complications could have come about—how communities of hunters, fishermen or farmers might have been developed into the colossus of our present public life. The schemes are probably not good history; the structuring, the reflexiveness of practice upon practice seems to be more complicated than we know. Still, the schemes have helped us to isolate the most basic features of practicality, to see its difficulties, and to say what the good of it can be.

Practice is finally brutal. There is sheer coercion in it, and resistance to coercion. Practice is here and now, as one individual wrests with another through that in him which shows itself as here and now. The brutality of practice can be attenuated from time to time; in long-range practice, for example, or in a society when we act practically through representatives; but then our practice is brutal in our agencies. Someone has to kill the cow, tear the fruit from the vine, cut down the tree, lay hands upon an enemy. No matter how reasonable we are, no matter how much compassion there is, no matter our finesse, the things of the world are not all rhymed in good accord, and we have finally to seize some of them, turn them to our account, and take from them what we need. Not everything is responsive to persuasion, not everything gives itself to us in love. Things do not even yield themselves through and through to discerning rationality; it is not true that one who cuts along the joints does not dull his knife. In the last extremity of practice we say to one another that you shall be killed if this is not done, and at our best in practice we are only at a small remove from this extreme. There is finally no removing all brutalities. If we become consummate in practice, we may reduce them some and not have them brutalize so much of us. But while reducible, refinable, all the brutalities of practice cannot be removed.

Many of us lose our feel for the brutalities of practice because the harshest ones take place on the edges of our communities. This is not so true for the poor, the uncomforted ill, or the otherwise oppressed. Practicalities for them are not distant, hidden, or indirect, though until recently they have not seen who they have mainly to oppose or how. Harshness is so hidden from those of us who are insulated that we may not even acknowledge our responsibility in it. Our own practical problems are, by comparison, problems of luxury, often delicate and tinged with privacy. But however protected or insulated we are, we are always in part defined as over against something else. We and that something else need not destroy one another, but the opposition is always there.

The strain of the opposition is also obscured by the fact that in much of our practice machines have become our consorts. It is an old story that once our tools were recognizably extensions of ourselves, that we used ourselves in using them and that our aim in using them was immediate and under our most direct control. Now, more or less self-contained in power, some machines are almost independent of us. In fact, they make demands on us, or partisans of them do—as if it would be impractical not to use the machines or not to use what they can be used to make, whether in more urgent practice such use satisfies our needs or not. Fad and fashion are signs that we have not specified our aim or that our preferences have not been stabilized as parts of it. The idly or conspicuously decorative or distracting merely decorates and distracts; it does not enhance a life.

More serious, of course, are those demands of our machines which dull our minds, our spirits and sensitivity. Consummate practicality provides place for our fullness as men. A practicality which does not, however masterful, is not practical enough; it is decadent, profane or effete. Machines which insulate us from the things they deal with can make us neglect the fact that it is we who deal with those things through the machines; they can even make us lose sight of what we are dealing with them for. We are then close to the end of our practicalities. It is no saving for us to become Luddites or to call for a return to direct and primitive brutalities. But except as we sense the brutalities even in attenuated practice, we will not deal with things effectively.

A soldier who kills another at a distance of a mile has still to see that he has killed a man, that he is a killer for all his technicality; and despite our own still greater distance, we have to acknowledge him as our agent and assume with him the responsibility. Both he and we will otherwise be less than we can be and more dangerous to others and ourselves. We can drive an opponent into a better practicality of his own which will lead him to find a way to overcome the jeopardies we make for him. The same is true inside a community. Marx thought that as one class oppressed another it gave the other the weapons with which to topple the oppressing class. Whether or not a society should be understood in terms of these classes, the grim truth of Marx's claim is that we blindly breed brutal oppositions, become insensitive to them, lose ingenuity in confronting them and have then to become more brutal in return. Only those who are well-to-do can be patient in the present. The rest, impatient, cannot be oppressed for very long. Even saints, pressed far enough, will try to change the world. What needs changing in the world, what the new oppositions are, on behalf of whom they are to be taken up, are nowadays said to be hard to see, especially if we are insulated from the most direct of practicalities. Closed in, our public lives are lived more and more through instruments which separate us from those with whom we have to deal. We drive and fly and phone and watch television, we use the mails and pay by check and have switches in the walls of the homes we feel little need to leave. For those of us who are not practical, this insulation is relief. For those of us who are, there is a deadening of ourselves and of the world.

Practice can in principle provide for the whole man, or the struggle in practice is to have it so. There have seemed to be two grand directions in which this fullness can be brought about. The

Athenians were the masters of one of them. They supposed that, at their fullest, men share a public life. In public, in the *polis,* they deal with the issues which concern free men—law and war and peace, heritage, fresh virtue and excellence. Slaves and women and children who are not free or able enough to have a say about these things do not have full lives. Free men talk with one another; they have something to talk about, and action comes ideally when it comes from speech. Speech is the stuff and structure of the public world. That world is perfected, for the Greeks, when men are virtuous enough to be moved by words alone. One does not talk with slaves or women, or even much with children, though young men are to learn both to listen and to speak. Private lives are public ones, shrunken in scope, decayed into lesser practicalities, conducted in silences. Together, in a community, the Greeks thought that the grossest practicalities could be overcome. Their genius was to see that when this has been done, their community need not decay, that still greater goods can be achieved, but that now their being together had to be sustained, not by brutal exertions, but by the less brutal commonalities which men who are freed from necessities can share best in talk.

The other great direction in which we have tried in practice to provide for the fullness of men does not share this Greek passion for the effectiveness, the lucidity, the grace and propriety of speech. Instead, it leads to speech becoming more and more private and less meaningful. This other direction sees practice, shared or not, as confronting the most insistent brutalities and then leaving men free to turn to satisfactions in more private lives. In public, if men talk at all, they ask one another to do things, they contract for doing them, and agree and report on their being done. They exhort and command and acknowledge compliance. When nothing needs to be done, there is no need for talk. Platitude and poetry do not affect one's dealings with the world; they may not even enhance private lives, given over as they are to less strenuous but especially precious practicalities. When there is little threat and jeopardy, a man can retire to enjoy and refine his own effectiveness. There are work benches, gardens, hobbies—things men like to do. Practical life should make room and resource enough for a man to do what he likes. Work is a public means to provide for his privacies. Even public service is a job.

Practice, then, can make our whole lives public, or it can preserve for us precious privacies. Where the Greeks saw us fulfilled and perfected mainly on our public side, nowadays most of us seem to think that our fullness comes in private life—it being ambiguous both for the Greeks and for ourselves what place there should be for learning, art and piety. The fullness of practice, the good of it, is in being together with every kind of thing. Every kind of fullness for men is in being together with other things: knowing them, enjoying them, contemplating them, worshiping and loving them. These activities, as goods, are themselves ways of being together with things, and practice is distinctively a way of being with things too. Those who see practice only as a means to something else want the unions it effects to lead to our being together with things in different and, as they think, better ways. There is no neutral ground, however, on which practice is rightly always to be a means to something else. In practice, we deal with all there is. We do so practically. Other ways of dealing with things are no more excellent. Practice can be informed, efficient and persistent, it can be a discerning, enjoyed, beneficent mastery of things. It need not be shortsighted, blundering, or blind. Through it, all of our dimensions can be used and brought together, so that as whole men we are together with the whole of things.

There is no name nowadays for the excellence in consummate practice. The Greeks called it "virtue," and they were clear in claiming that practice can fulfill a man. Pericles, for example, claimed for the Athenians that while they are "the most daring in action," they are also "most given to reflection upon the ventures we mean to undertake," that in contrast, for less virtuous men, "boldness means ignorance and reflection brings hesitation." So too in their virtue, Pericles said that the Athenians are "lovers of beauty with no extravagance and lovers of wisdom without weakness." All the parts of men are used in a public life; and we "regard the man who takes no part in public affairs, not as one who minds his own business, but as good for nothing." We would perhaps not make this judgment now. Our own point, however, would be the same: that practice can use all of us, that all our dimensions enter into doing it, though when they do, they are shaped or configured in a certain way. There are other ways of using ourselves and dealing with the world, but none is better than practicality. None uses us more fully or masters more of things. Practice, in its excellence, is an excellent enterprise for men, an excellent way of dealing with everything. It does not contain all the virtues of every other mode of activity, but then the others do not have its effectiveness. It is a basic way of dealing with the whole of things, and a man of practice is thereby as important, as valuable, as any other kind of man.

The world in practice is forever filled with dangers. We cannot dominate much or for very long. To come to his dominion, to make the world yield what we need, a man of practice often needs support from men of other kinds. A scientist, a philosopher, an artist or religious man is often of use to him. It too often happens, though, that a man of practice will misunderstand these other kinds of men. He will suppose that since they are of use to him, they are really men of practice too, only not so direct, so forceful, or so effective as he himself can be. Many a man of practice talks about scholars, artists and religious men as if they had retreated into thinner practicalities because they do not have his grit, stubbornness and virility. They are weak, and if the times are not urgent, they have to be protected. Practical men will then serve with generosity as trustees of colleges, directors of museum boards, and as vestrymen and church councilors, even if they do not quite see what knowledge, art and religion are.

When the demands of practice are urgent, the man of practice who makes the practical mistake of supposing that other kinds of men are also really practical will be less patient and make more stern demands. He will insist that since the so-called other kinds of men are really practical, they should serve the aimed concern of practice too. He thinks he sees that concern most clearly, without the castes of paler thought and gentle grace and piety. He therefore acts as if practice defines the role of reason, the end that art shall serve and the service that faith can practically demand. For such a shortsighted man of practice, in the urgency of practice, scientists become technicians, philosophers are to justify practice in ideology, artists are propagandists, and religion is a consolation to those who are victimized by the burliness of things. The concern of practice, he thinks, is best served by him. He may even think of himself, or want others to think of him, as the model for other sorts of men, a master thinker-artist-prophet who is effective too.

The impracticality of this mistake comes out when other sorts of men insist on the distinctness of their own concerns, when they say that they need not deal with everything in the way the man of practice does. Should the man of practice persist in his mistake, he will find ways in practice to put down the revolts. Thinkers, artists, pious men will be charged as subversives, cranks and heretics, and they will not be supported practically. Narrow practice will not tolerate thinkers who are thought to threaten its security; it will not allow for artists who are said to incite us to irresponsibility, and it will not allow for religious men who transgress from church to state. Should men of reason, art and faith claim that practice does not rule for them, some practical men will regard their claim as a threat—and it may in fact be a threat if the domain which practice has won is too narrow to allow for a fullness for all the kinds of men. An excellent man of practice would then try to enlarge that domain. One who is not excellent will try to retain it as it is and turn to settle what he takes to be revolt. This course is at last not very practical.

Practice is hard and harsh even when it is done well and not shortsightedly. It is filled with hazard. Each moment is a fresh trial, and past successes are guides only to a point. It is a world or a way of getting at the world to which some men are suited naturally. They are practical men, and they are good at practice, more or less. Some will risk the widest challenges and persist in the face of all defeats. They are the heroes even though their victories are never complete. Other practical men are more cautious and less venturesome; they do not recover well from their defeats and they restrain and circumscribe their practicalities. In dreams and reverie they still conjure themselves as great men. They may mull on the mistakes and mischance that did not put them in the right place at the right time, and then they explain to their sons that this is the way of the world and that smaller practicalities can also satisfy a man.

The most poignant cases are those in which men take themselves to be practical but find out that all along they were men of a different kind. It is not always clear to a man what kind of man he is. Usually, it takes a crisis for him to find out, but even then it can happen that he will never surely know. Men who are really practical feel themselves to be practical even when they are defeated by the world. Others, faced with failures, may feel that they were never really practical at all. They are not converted from being practical into being another kind of man. What happens is that they discover that they were never really practical but that they only thought of themselves that way.

Think, for instance, of Shaw's play, *The Devil's Disciple*. Dick Durgeon sees himself as a worldly man of practical ingenuities, but at a crisis point he discovers that he is a religious man and that he was so all along. Or take genuine examples: St. Francis or St. Ignatius, soldiers who found themselves to be religious men. Or the Galilean fishermen or Gauguin or Faraday or Shaw himself, the efficient clerk, or all the corporation presidents who have turned from business to become teachers, writers or monks. These examples show that when men who are not really practical find that they cannot maintain themselves in what looks like practice, they come to believe that they were misplaced, that they were really men of reason all along, or that they were artists or religious men. They are the same now as they always were; only they see more clearly who they are. They will sometimes talk with bitterness and contempt about the way they used to go at things, about the foolishness, ugliness or sacrilege of their lives. They may even try to persuade other men that practice is all vanity. Their failure at practice showed them what kinds of men they are. They feel at last restored and they think of themselves as aimed, not at a mastery of things through a course of time, but in a concern of a very different kind.

Chapter III

The Life of Reason

―――――――

THE REACH OF KNOWLEDGE

Men of reason try to understand the world—to know what things there are, what there must be, and what can come about. They aim to catch the whole of things in understanding them. They also aim to make these things more rational. There are, they think, no surds which stand beyond the reach of thought. Here and there, of course, there are errors and mistakes, and there are dark places we have not see through as yet. These, however, are faults and failures on our part. With persistence and better use of mind, they can be overcome. There is nothing we cannot come to understand.

What men of reason want to know is, simply, everything—not merely what there is right now or what happened in the past, but all that there could ever be or ever have to be. Different men of reason set about this knowing from different starting points and proceed in different ways. Some begin from what happened in the past; others build from what they know of the present, trying then to think what must have been the case for things to be this way just now; still others start from what has always to be true or from what is merely possible. Wherever they begin, men of reason have the same aim: to reach by reasoning into absolutely everything, to know what has always and everywhere to be the case and to penetrate to things by seeing them as cases of a principle which is lucid to our rationality.

The knowledge at which men of reason aim has to be acquired, but not by starting from total ignorance. Were we ignorant of everything, we would not know that we were ignorant. We would have no place from which to start the search of knowledge; we would know of no direction in which to go; there would be nothing we were looking for, no method by which to find it out, and no way of recognizing, even if we came to know it, that it is what we need to know. Ignorance cannot be sheer and idle emptiness.

We know something when we are ignorant. Our ignorance is like an aching gap or a darkness in what we already know. We want the gap filled in, the darkness lighted up; we want to know still more. It was only in Eden and even there not for very long that ignorance was bliss. We see or are made to see that we are ignorant, and as we know that we are ignorant, we know what it is that we need to know more about. To acquire this further knowledge, we have to have a place to start—with what we already know. We also know what sort of thing we are looking for. We are therefore able to recognize it when we acquire it. Because of the connection between what we already know and what we are ignorant of, there are methods by which we can make our way. Our starting place in knowing is rich enough to show us what we are looking for, the direction in which we have to go, and the steps we will have to take along the way.

We should notice, however, that if we have to know something in order to find out about something else, not everything we know can have been found out. Something has to serve us at the start; something has to serve us as a start. It is true of course that once we have acquired knowledge, what we have learned can help us as we go further on. But not all our knowledge can have been acquired in such a way. We must possess some knowledge natively

—not that it is clear to us at first or that we have much control in using it. But unless there were some knowledge at "the start" we could have no understanding of the processes of coming to know or even of being taught. We come to know through something we already know. What we know most basically is hard to isolate. Still, some men, as we will see, try to make it clear.

We should also notice that when we acquire knowledge, we do not leave behind the place from which we start. Knowing, finding out, is not a journey from place to separate place. We start with knowing something and we go on to know still more. But in the process we do not "forget" what we already know. What we know is carried into what we come to know; it leads us into it. It may even come to be more lucid to us there. What we have to know in order to know something else is therefore never lost to us. It does not become more remote, but may, instead, become more plain or clear.

In these last observations, there are two specially important points: (1) that our native and basic knowledge shall be rich enough to lead us into everything we could ever come to know, and (2) that if what we know at first is not left behind or lost but is carried into what we come to know, then, in the setting of our acquired knowledge, it may seem to us more clear; it may be more definite and have its lead lines shadowed out, or perhaps it is only that we come to such circumspection through our knowing that we can see it better later on. Whichever is the case, our basic knowledge is not beyond our reach: we can recover it, "remember" it; we can try to set it out.

It is with our basic knowledge that philosophers are most concerned. They want to know what things there have to be and what knowledge is beyond all question sure. They care little for this or that specific fact, unless it is a plain clue to what is more basic in our knowledge or the world. They suppose that by thinking through what we already know they can isolate what they are looking for. If it is true that basic knowledge is carried into everything we come to know, then, of course, it is sound to claim that it can be recovered there. No experiments, no expeditions, no laboratories are therefore needed for philosophic thought. One need only think about what we already know, or about philosophy itself, the idea of trying to recover what is basic to all thought.

It is as if thought pressed far enough, pressed on by its own demand, will lead to our seeing and setting out the basis of our thoughts. In whatever way it is done—by going over, under, through, or into our more familiar thought—however well it is done or with what consensus among philosophers, the aim of philosophers has been to get reflective hold on our most basic thoughts. Being clear about our basic knowledge is knowing philosophically.

Our basic knowledge, philosophic knowledge, is about absolutely everything. We come to the specialized knowledge we acquire through what we already know, and what we know is then carried further on. Our basic knowledge must, therefore, be large and supple enough to enable us to acquire specialized knowledge; but then, to state the point again, while we acquire this knowledge by going through and beyond our basic thought, we do not go away from it. Our basic knowledge, to use the word that was used before, is the Good, or our grasp of it, or its hold on us. In our specialized knowing, what we do is to see how what we confront and want to know is already qualified by the Good; then, out of our concern for it through the Good, we qualify it still more.

How our basic knowledge is connected with what it enables us to know is one of the most debated of philosophical questions. The question is set out, never innocently, in different formulations. How is the abstract related to the concrete? How are forms or essences or species or categories related to contents, existents, individuals or the manifold of sense? What has the *a priori* to do with our knowledge of contingent fact? There are still other ways of setting the question and, naturally, there is variety in the answers too. There have been mainly four sorts of answers, depending on whether that through which we know is said to be the same or of the same nature as what we finally know or not. The answers are different interpretations of the Good, or of what is like it in helping us to know.

(1) Hegelians think that all we can come to know is wholly contained in our basic philosophical conceptions. We cannot readily deduce our specialized knowledge from the conceptions. Still, what we come to know is the same as our first knowledge, only specified by the terms of that knowledge itself. What seems,

then, to be abstract and philosophical only seems that way when first it is found in mind. Later on, as we become more clear in knowing and more clear about what it is to know, it loses this first appearance and is seen to be concrete. There is no separation between that through which we come to know and what we come to know itself. They are the same, only the abstractness of the first appearances is gone.

This view of knowledge would be inescapable if there were but one dimension in the real. Were knowledge possible in such a world, what makes for rationality would be the same as what is real. What is real would be all rational; it could be nothing else. The world, however, is not quite so homogeneous, and that is why there are difficulties in this view. Individuals, specific things, are more complicated than it is able to allow. There are indeed features of things which we understand and which, in turn, enable us to understand the things. But then there are also features of things which make them things *to be* understood, instances of principles, singulars not constituted wholly by what we know in general. A thing we come to know about has to be confronted, and the *it* in it, not its *it-ness,* is not fully general. We know of it through what may be found at any time or place. But the singularity which is then and there is not the same as that. The great argument in support of Hegel's view is that all our knowledge, and indeed every part of it, is unified. Although it seems plainly correct to insist upon the unities, it seems mistaken to suppose that they are owed to the sameness of that through which we know and the knowledge we come to have.

Will it do instead to hold (2) that what is finally known is altogether different in its nature from that through which we know? This is the view of Kantians, or neo-Kantians and conventionalists. They think that we come to know through forms and categories which make our knowledge possible, but then they also hold that the real has to be shaped by these instruments of ours—the real differs in nature from the forms. The root difficulty in this view is that it cannot explain how, or how without distortion, the real is known or made knowable through forms that are not natively its own. That through which we know is so different from what is to be known that the one cannot make the other knowable. Forms *for* a content have to be made to be the forms of it, and if a content has no form of its own, it either cannot be given one, or whatever one it is given, is given arbitrarily. Knowledge is thereby either impossible or so arbitrary that it is neither right nor wrong. If we separate radically that through which we are to know and that which is to be known, the two cannot in any way be joined.

(3) Will it do to say that we do not put forms into things but that, instead, they are already there, or that they are there at least in the things which occur in nature, and that when we come to know about them we simply apprehend the forms; we grasp them and come to have them in our minds. This is very like Aristotle's view. According to it, inquiry is a way of turning things or delving into them so that we can apprehend their forms. That through which we know is therefore the same as what we know, or it is *almost* the same. The small difference is what makes for the only difficulty on this view.

The difference is that something *has* a form but that its form is not the same as it, or not the whole of it. To know a thing, therefore, we must do more than grasp its form. We have to see the thing as having form; we have to see the form as the form of the very thing we understand. Can this be done by grasping, by apprehending forms? It seems that it cannot for the reason that the form of a thing is after all a form, and if one insists that it is *the* form of *this* thing, he has seen at best only that a form has been complicated some. There seems no getting through a form to see the thing of which it is a form. A form is all that we can grasp and, for those who take this view, it is our only access to understanding things. Even if we were somehow to see a form in a thing, since it is the form alone we grasp, the thing, as more than form, remains for us indefinite. We never penetrate it enough to understand it or to see it as a natured individual.

The great strength and good sense of this view is therefore hampered by the claim that it is only by the apprehension of a form that we know what something is. This seems only a part of our knowing it. The other part, as we will see, is to move not only through a form toward an individual, but also through an individual to a form. We combine by reasoning what we see along both these routes and are not content with apprehensions, graspings, all alone. Aristotle suggested something like this himself in the *Posterior Analytics*. Mainly, however, he confined himself to the one route, to claims about apprehending, seizing forms and having them in mind. This does not take us far enough.

(4) Finally, it does no good to claim that there is no Good, no knowledge through which we come to know of things. A number of philosophers in the empirical tradition have held this sort of view. Nothing, for them, mediates our knowing; no basic knowledge is the ground or instrument of our knowing other things. What we know is present to us; it is presented to us and that is all there is to that, except that we can combine and manipulate what remains in us after the presentations pass, and there are some expectations too. The difficulty here is that such data as we are given do not represent a thing. Unmediated, they are too self-contained to tell of something else; their occurrence and quality are not signs of anything. A Humean idea, for example, represents neither an entity apart from us nor even the impression of which it is the residue. It is entirely self-enclosed, so much so that we cannot even understand the cautious claim that an unknown something causes, in a way we cannot know, the occurrence of this idea in us right now. On this view, we do not know *about* things at all. It is not clear even that we know the ideas which occur in us. It is bold perhaps to be this skeptical. However, we contradict ourselves in holding that this is an account of knowledge or that it is true.

At every quarter, then, an understanding of knowledge seems badly blocked. Claim to acquire knowledge with or through the knowledge we already have and we have to justify this claim by showing how the acquisition can have come about. In this, however, our basic knowledge seems too thick, too thin, or too tightly self-enclosed. It is either the same as what we finally know, so that there is no going through it to something else, or it is so empty that its use is either impossible or unrestrained. It may also be that, while lucid in itself, it is so self-contained that it does not enable us to see that there are things which we understand. It is desperation, though, and no solution, to claim that we do not know of things at all.

There is, however, one turn which can still be made. The seeming blockages occur if we assume that in knowing we come at things along a single route. The insights of the four sorts of views which have been set out above are narrow sights, for this is what they claim. Even so, much in them can be preserved by noting, as we saw before, that in dealing with things through one dimension of the real, that one dimension plays a double role. What we will have to see is that we come at what we know along different routes, that we combine the results in reasoning, and that the combination is our construction, our knowledge of the world. This is the turning we have now to explore more fully.

We know or understand things when we see how they qualify the Good, when we represent the intelligible way in which they are together with others and other sorts of things. Should one say that this cannot be true, that it is incidental to a thing how it is along with others and that knowing it is really knowing it as all alone, he would misconstrue the natures of things, think of knowledge as impossible and, in effect, he would finally contradict himself. Every thing, every kind of thing, is what it is in part by being together with other things. No doubt things are also something on their own, or from their own side out. But were they all enclosed, cut off from others and from us, there would be no possibility of knowing them, and he who claimed to know them would oppose himself in saying that he had access to what he found to be inaccessible. Knowing things, understanding them, is seeing them in connection with other things, but not merely as one among the others, as if alongside of them. It is seeing them in one of the ways in which they are together with other things and seeing how they contribute to this unity. The unity we acknowledge in knowing things is the Good as specialized.

In knowing, we come at what we want to know more about along two different routes. (1) We acknowledge it as something we want to know more about, as something which we sense is qualified by the Good, though we do not see very fully how. Were the thing we want to know about a sheer, bare x, a thing as merely there, there would be no ground for thinking that there is something more to know. In fact, we would not even think of it at all; there would be nothing in an x of which we could have a thought. To approach something as a *that* about which we want to know still more, we represent it as something over against both us and other things in a certain way. Nothing can be separated from us, nothing can be an object about which we are to know still more, unless it is also together with us and other things. We know of this togetherness before we know more of what it is. This is what we want to know. (2) We also approach what we want to know more about through what we already know of it and through what we think could be true of it. We have a sense of the kind of sense that things must finally have. All our claims are sensible or not, and only what is judged as sensible is looked at as being true or false. The sense of things is the widest truth we know of them. We approach anything we want to know more about through our feel for the sense that must be specified in what we come to know. This feel for sense or rationality is our sight of things through the Good. What we are looking for is how the Good is specified. Coming to know more about a thing is the joining of these two approaches in a course of reasoning.

With limited accuracy, these two approaches can be described again by talking about subjects and predicates, though not in quite the usual way. Let us say that we represent what we want to know more about through a subject, and what we come to know about it will be represented by a predicate. The knowing, then, is the joining of the subject and the predicate. Both the subject and predicate have to be available, and both have to have a meaning before or as we come to know; they would otherwise have no meaning until they are joined in fact, and then that meaning could have come about only by a miracle. What we come to mean in knowing we must have already meant before. But knowledge is also an advance. The advance, as we will have to see, is that in the course of coming to know more about a thing, the meanings of both the available subject and the predicate are modified. Were this not the case, knowledge would not be acquired. It would at best be a recovery of what we already know and mean, or a combination of these things. New knowledge has, however, to be produced and made to be ours. This can only be done by modifying what we already mean, and this is done in reasoning. These claims require, of course, a special understanding of the notions of "subject," "predicate," and especially of "reasoning."

Most accounts of argument do not share this view. They hold that meanings do not change in argument. There is deduction, so it is claimed, where a predicate which appears in a premiss occurs in the conclusion too—the same predicate, meaning the same. Were it to mean something else, what was meant in the premiss could not, it is said, be a good reason for believing what we conclude. Then, there is what is called induction, where a predicate which appears in the premisses is applied in the same sense to subjects different from the ones which are mentioned there. Without this sameness of meaning throughout, the claim is that there could be no reasoning.

The trouble with this claim is that it has either nothing or else very little to do with reasoning. It is a claim about argument, and an argument is not a piece of reasoning. It is a construction designed by logicians for the purpose of making prominent something of the wholeness or unity which is found in completed reasoning. There are different logics, different theories about the unity of an argument. It is rightly an important point of many of the theories that what is meant in an argument shall stay the same throughout, so as not to intrude upon or complicate the form. But argument is one thing and reasoning is another. In reasoning our meanings are modified and changed. Coming to know is not heaping together and rearranging what we already with fixity mean. This is what is supposed only by those who take knowledge to be a combination of definite ideas and reasoning to be a construction out of fixed claims. Reasoning is coming to mean more (more specifically or more generally) than we meant before we inquired; it is a joining of our meanings together so as to make more definite the kinds of meaning that enter into a final claim. These, when achieved, are read (and rightly so) into an argument as its constant terms. In the reasoning, however, the meanings did not have this constancy.

One premiss, if that be the word, will be the subject term. It is a shrunken claim, or one that is indefinite: "this is a—a something or other"; "this tree is—I know not—what." In either case, the subject term does not represent what we want to know more about as all complete. There is perhaps a minimum that can be represented through a subject (some philosophers talk of ultimate subjects), and there is perhaps a maximum (which is the opinion, for example, of the theologians who claim that all that can be said of God is said in the calling of his name). But whatever the extremes, subjects isolate our subject by representing it through those respects in which it is such as to specify the Good. They do not set out for us how the Good is specified. Subjects leave that indefinite.

A predicate, if we can use that word, sets before us the Good as specified. It too is a shortened or unsettled claim: "something is a tree, or is perhaps a tree." We have some sight of the predicates we can use to know more about a thing before we make use of them in fact. Were we to get at things only through the Good, we would know too little of those things specifically; perhaps we would not even know that there are things to know. Were we able to get at them only through confronting them, we would also know little about them, perhaps not even that there is something more to know. Because we can get at things through two accesses at least, we can find out more of what they are. We do this by colligating our premises—the ones we have found— feeling for a middle term and refining the meanings of the other terms. This process of adjusting meanings is done with an eye both to satisfying the urgent ignorance that led us into inquiry and to the fullest sense of things. It leads to a conclusion that is both sensible and, such as we have reason to think, true. Combined in reasoning, the routes through subjects and predicates are the way in which we know, or know more about, individuals. Together, they incorporate and preserve much of the insight in the four accounts of knowledge that were sketched before. We will have to see that this is so. But more should be said at first about the route to knowledge through predicates. Predicates, more than subjects, occupy those who reflect about knowledge. They represent the *what* in what it is we know. What shall we understand this *what* to be, and how is it represented? Even if only in brief outline, something should be said about these themes.

It is sure that the predicates of individuals do not represent a mere surface sensuosity. In knowing, on all accounts of it, we remove, submerge, or set aside the sensuosities of experience. Their closeness, their here and nowness, the idiosyncrasy of their being ours, is too rich for knowledge to accommodate. We try in knowing to offset the peculiarities of our special way of getting at the things we come to know so that other men can assent or not to what we finally claim. We can do this only if the sensuous does not intrude too much.

Nor does it seem that a predicate can represent a definite potentiality or a property which is hidden by or buried beneath all that shows on the surface of a thing. Were there such potentialities, we could never find them out or understand what the words which stand for them are supposed to mean; were there such properties, we could never see them as the properties of individuals. Under the surfaces of things, such potentialities or properties are too removed from things or are too inaccessible to show us the *what* of whatever things there are.

In knowing about the individuals that are around us now, then, we can neither stay with their sensuosities nor move entirely away from them. The great Kantian mid-position is that predicates stand for rules or orderings of appearances. For reasons which have already been explored, it is unlikely that Kant's view will finally do: the orderings are either inapplicable or arbitrary. If we turn Kant's view around, however, if we turn it upside down, near to the way in which Peirce saw that it could and should be turned, we will have a different mid-position which is more nearly right. Instead of having predicates stand for sensuosities ordered by a mind engaged in representing things, we will see that in the activity of the things we come to know about there is a law or an order or a regularity. We come to understand it in the course of our own experience, and we represent it as we are ourselves engaged in an ordered course of inquiry. This is the sort of thing we have to say if we think of things as qualified by the Good and of ourselves as knowing them through the access which the Good itself provides. What, in outline, are the main claims of such a view?

Individuals are not all surface now. Nor have they a set of shaped, submerged potentialities. Still, pressed by time into new present moments, individuals nevertheless come to deal with what is about them in a more distinctive way. We, for example, appropriate an overriding time, press out against others and move inward to consolidate ourselves. The Good, as it is found in individuals, is the way in which all of this is done. It is in the nature of a law, our law, or law as ours, law in an individual; it is a nature active in a lawlike way. It is this law in things which predicates represent.

This law, this nature, this Good in things—since it has to do with individuals being together with other sorts of things—is portioned by or enters into different temporalities. It has to do with the sheerly present, with the promise of what is to come and with binding necessity as well. It is not something we see only when we look back upon what has already occurred. We also take account of it when we predict. It enters even into the confrontations of a present, underlying sensuosities, and the order in the place it makes for individuals is read by some, and rightly, as a mark of our connectedness with God.

This will have no sense if, again, we make the mistake of supposing that individuals are whole and all complete and located at a present in an overarching time. If we see things, though, as helping to create the presentness of a moment and as standing, even then, in connection with a nontransient being, it will be no surprise that there is both persistence and regularity in the course of what occurs. Nor should it then be surprising to find that what predicates represent should have been interpreted in so many different ways—as standing for forms or essences, or for potentialities or powers, or for emasculated sensuosities, or for unities of possible sense experience, even for conventionalities. Each of these views is plausible, only each is distorted by its narrow sight. It takes account of but one feature of the unity which the Good provides in things.

The plausibilities of these foreshortened views can be preserved by seeing that the Good, the whole of it, not a portion of it, is specified in individuals and that there it qualifies all the dimensions of an individual's activity. It accounts for what is intelligible in things with respect to God (species nature, so to speak), for the distinctiveness in our appropriations of passing time (development, so to say); it accounts even for things being understandable as they exist against others now, as they specify the Good and press against the others who specify it too. It is the Good, then, or the Good as it is specified in things, which is represented by our predicates. Forms, sensuosities and futurities are but portioned aspects of the Good. They show how the Good, as in a thing, qualifies the thing's being together with transience, with other individuals, with God and, in its double role, with the Good itself. Each of these is a sort of unity, a sameness of quality, for example, or a unity of a subject, or a singleness for occurrences. Together, they are a predicate of an individual.

Were it not for the double role of the Good, were it not for the fact that we can discern the Good through individuals and see them as shadowed out through it, there could be no knowledge, no representation, no subjects or no predicates. An individual can be indicated by a subject because we can, in acknowledging it, acknowledge it as a locus of the Good. In the case of a predicate, going to a thing through the Good, we discern the Good as specified and see it, therefore, as something which we already know, though not in good detail. Philosophers, so the saying goes, are not surprised by anything. The rationale for this is simply that they are concerned to see the Good and not to find it new in special cases, even when it is detailed. There are, however, special cases of the Good, and whether they are of interest to philosophers or not, they can be set out or signified. One can show another who already has some hold upon the Good how, in a case he is directed to, the Good that he already knows takes on a special guise. We can move toward more and more specialized cases, holding as fixed a certain view of and through the Good. This seems to be what happens in our specialized theoretical knowledge. Or we can try more and more to see the Good itself, to make out as far as we ever can, its configuration and its bearing upon other sorts of things. This is what is done in philosophical knowledge.

Men try in philosophy to move toward seeing the Good by getting at the final sense of what we already know, the sense that whatever we can come to know will also have to have. They try to isolate it through what we know, to have it, as it were, alone, and to see how it makes for the sense of everything. Philosophers, or good ones, are therefore always teetering on the edge of sense. They are steadied here and there by the firmest of our general conceptions; but then, they are unsettled, pushed further, by discerning that even in our most ranging thought there are suppositions which have still to be thought through and justified. They aim for that last refuge of all our questions about what is true and meaningful. "This is true only if this or that is so"—and so on, but not without an end. "We can understand this or make out the meaning of that only if we first see the meaning of something else, and something else"—but again, not without an end. The finalities of truth and meaning which these principles suggest, the one finality in whose terms all else is to be understood, is ironically never fully clear to us. We see it and through it only unsteadily. The world, for philosophers, will one day seem all lucid, no part of it unclear; on another, nothing seems in the least to make revealing sense.

The reason for this inescapable unsettlement is that the Good is not finally fixed and self-contained. It is itself qualified by other sorts of things, by God and time and by things which are like ourselves. It does not itself undergo a change; it is not wholly subject to the strains of transience, but its pertinence to other things is altered some and its coloring can shift. No matter the excellence of mind, neither the Good nor the world as seen through it can be sighted with steady lucidity. There is no dimension of things that can be mastered with finality. We know this to be true for practice; it is never without an end. Even saintliness is at every point specked a bit and flawed, and works of art do not exhaust all that beauty could ever be. The same is true in knowing and understanding things. We have therefore to see that a sound approach to the whole of things through the Good is not had in a momentary grasp of things but in the making of a life in thought. This will be a life of reason, and we should try to say what this life is. Before we turn to the excellence which such a life provides, it might be of use to see its perverted contrast, a nearly sound view of the life of reason exaggerated into falsity. This is the view, dear and horrifying, parallel to the exaggerated claim for practicality, that it is only through the Good that we can deal with the whole of things and that philosophers, therefore, should have dominion over other men and things. What lends such strong credence to this view? What is its contaminating irrationality?

THE DOMINION OF REASON

There is nothing we cannot know about; nothing lies beyond all reach of reasoning. The reason for this is that everything is affected by the Good and it is through our hold of the Good that we come to know of other things. They are not as lucid to us as the Good itself can come to be, but we can know about them even so. We may in fact be led to do more than that: we may want to change them, to relocate them, to have the Good which is specified in them be made still more prominent and plain.

The Good in a thing is a way in which the thing is together with other sorts of things, including the Good itself. An individual, however, can be out of joint with itself, and with others and other sorts of things. Plato talks about a right order for the soul in which each part has its function and does not intrude upon the function of the other parts. A badly ordered soul, he thinks, is in conflict with itself; it also faces other things improperly. In the same way, then, a man of reason may look at himself and other things and judge that he and they do not incorporate the Good as clearly as they might. There is perhaps not as firm a hold on time as there might be; perhaps too much of us is caught in opposition and restraint; perhaps we are overly preoccupied with God. Whatever the imbalance, for a man of reason the Good is the measure of how things ought to be. He thinks of himself as a spokesman for the Good. He is, as Santayana says, in love with it. He sees where and how it is obscured, or where it has not been brought out yet. He may even make himself its instrument and try to have the whole of things brought to the Good for governance. It is for him as if the measure of the togetherness of things were provided by the Good alone.

The motives on which men have undertaken to have things more fully show the Good differ with their views of the Good itself. In the image of the cave in *The Republic,* for example, Plato supposes that a man can come on his own, apart from a community, to see the sun, the Good, and that once he has seen it, he will want to go on contemplating it. He knows the Good; that is enough for him. The Good does not require that he reform the world. If we think of the Good as Plato does, as not needing anything itself, then those who see it do not have to act on its behalf: there is no reason for the man who knows the Good to do anything to have it brought out better in the world.

Plato, however, tries to persuade the philosopher, the man who has seen the Good, to return to the cave to lighten it. The philosopher is not a Jesus or a Buddha who turns to men in love. He loves the Good, not other men, not even the Good in them, and

71

given what Plato thinks the Good to be, his persuasion cannot be very strong. What arguments should move the philosopher to return to the cave? In one argument, Plato says that he is in debt to the men who are confined in it. This is not strong enough. Even if the philosopher is in their debt, what shows the debt to be so great that it should be repaid at so great a cost? Besides, how would trying to make the Good more clear be repaying it? In another place, image left aside, Plato's argument is that no man can completely escape the cave; we are always touched by politics. Even though the Good, then, does not require us to act on its behalf, the question is whether we will be ruled by men who are worse than us or not. This is the argument that the man who has seen the Good should rule because, otherwise, lesser men will rule. What is the bad in this? Perhaps it is that corrupt rule will intrude even on the philosopher. But this is too thin, too petulant and too personal an argument. It may be that whoever undertakes to rule should do so reluctantly; even then, though, there should be a positive reason for the undertaking. Plato, with the Good as all complete and contemplatable, cannot provide for one. None of his arguments is strong. Still, persuasive or not, because of what the philosopher knows, Plato thinks that he is the only one suited to the responsibility of rule.

On a view of the Good which is different from Plato's, there can be positive motives for seeking to rule. Whether they are sound or not, we will consider soon. One such view, close to the view which has been argued in the text, is that while the Good has to be discerned, it does not stand off alone. It can be got at through the things around us now. Searching for the Good, trying to know it, could then lead to an experiment, a politics. Why try to reform the world? Why, to know the Good. The urge to know is the motive for effecting changes in the world. Ruling is thereby not a distracting burden. It is an opportunity to know the Good more fully than before. Plato's philosopher already knows the Good and therefore has no reason to turn aside from knowing it to rule. For one, however, who has literally to make it out, the desire to know is the motive in all acts.

Something like this motive is described by Skinner in *Walden Two,* though Skinner does not found it on a notion of the Good. A visitor to the Walden community has been talking about the "extensive research" needed to get a really large-scale science of behavior under way. Frazier, one of the community's planners, responds by saying that the visitor has described the

> *only* side of Walden Two that really interests me. To make men happy, yes. To make them productive in order to insure the continuation of that happiness, yes. But what else? Why, *to make possible a genuine science of human behavior.* These things aren't for the laboratory. They're not "academic questions." What an apt expression! They concern our very lives! We can study them only in a living culture, and yet a culture which is under experimental control. Nothing short of Walden Two will suffice. It must be a real world, this laboratory of ours; and no foundation can buy a slice of it.

The point is that, if we think of the Good as implicated in the being of other sorts of things, the passion to know it need not keep us in a narrow life. It can, as one example, be the passion in a kind of politics, with the politics a part of knowing things, not something separate on its own. We can then see ourselves as acting on behalf of the Good in the very course of coming to know it.

There can no doubt be other motives too, depending on how the Good is viewed or misconstrued. On each, with reluctance or impatiently, men of reason try to make the whole of things more rational. Their persistent criticism is that things are done foolishly, stupidly, inconsistently. They see the mistakes and know what things ought to be. They know they know more than other men, but then their extravagance is unreasonably to say that knowledge of and through the Good shall be the measure of all things. For many a man of reason, not Faust alone, the passion to know becomes the lust to be master of the world.

A man of reason who makes this mistake will also mistakenly suppose that other kinds of men are really men of reason too, only weaker in their reasoning and not so very clear. He may think that, unlike men of practice, he really knows what he is striving for; he thinks that he can exhibit it in surer ways than lesser artists can, and he is sure that what he seeks is worthiest of trust. These other men, he thinks, should serve the Good as it is seen by him. They should do what he tells them to—arrange the means and carry out the plans that he has made; they should help through works of imagination which aim to make men more sensitive to the order that reason achieves most perfectly; or they are to set the most subtle truths in forms that will prompt devotions from people who would not otherwise know what to do. Those who are not reasonable enough to be persuaded of what they should do are then known for what they are: balky men of affairs are brute and unthinking; artists are irrational and dangerous because they cannot explain their work in reason's terms or control the visions which they stir; finally, religious men know no reasoned truths and have forsaken argument for mystery. One has only to read Plato's *Republic* to see the places the knowing king assigns to less reasonable men and to see, as well, who is expelled from and dishonored by the state.

These observations are of course stressed to extreme. The aim they exaggerate, however, is not an uncommon one. The view of many a man of reason is that sound policy comes from a sound theory and that he, of course, is the one who can delve and turn and think the issues through. Having seen what they are, or what is the Good in them, he can consider how the Good can be made more prominent. Policy is his directive on how this shall be done. It is to be carried out by men less reasonable than himself, the directive serving as their rationality, and its generality will depend on the thoughtfulness of the men it is given to. Some will need only the barest of directions; they can see how policy is to be implemented in wide varieties of circumstance. Others need full routines: "when this happens, this is to be done." The consummate man of reason himself needs no directive, no routines. He sees himself as responsive to the Good anywhere, everywhere, and through it his way with things, he thinks, is clear. He sees his rule as benign and persuasive, dominion following the gentle insinuations of rationality. For those in whom there is little reason, persuasion has, of course, a more coercive form. Those who will not be moved by the thoughts of him who has thought of everything will be moved by the forces he knows how to control.

The vision of the reason's dominion, animating many men of thought, has often been opposed by men who, of course, seem to the man of reason too irrational. Thrasymachus thrashes against Plato's view of justice, but Plato has arranged *The Republic* so that Thrasymachus is arguing for a narrowed version of Plato's own view and, predictably, he contradicts himself. Kierkegaard testifies to what, beyond reason, men have finally to be committed to. And there have been many claims that we are free beyond all restraints even though our freedom is an absurdity. What is said to stand outside of reason cannot be seen as anything except irrational. Still, it is a mistake, even an irrationality, to claim that reason properly has dominion over everything. To see the mistake—not merely to rail against it—is to see that while nothing is outside the reach of reason, what reason gets at can be got at in other ways as well. The strongest argument on behalf of the sovereignty of reason is that reason can adjudicate with right regard the competing claims of things. It can indeed adjudicate them; but the mistake is in supposing that reason's adjudication is the only way in which things can be brought to unity. Reason itself, our sense for and through the Good, should show that this is so.

Several lines of thought can bring this out. The simplest and perhaps the most persuasive one shows that the kind of unity which things have as they specify the Good is not their only unity, that another sort of unity is even then supposed, and that the unity which the Good provides is neither the only nor the best community that things can have. Many spokesmen for the Good would, of course, deny that this is so. But their denials, as we will see, depend on false premises or inconsistent arguments. A defense of even an extravagant reason ought to be reasonable at least.

Think again, then, for example, of Plato's view of us in *The Republic*. According to Plato, we have reason, spirit and appetite. Spirit and appetite are said to be selfish powers, concerned only with their own satisfactions, not for the whole of the soul. Reason takes account of the whole of us. It is therefore the only power in us which can assign to spirit and appetite and to itself the right and proper roles. But then, notice that Plato also talks about a disordered or unordered soul. How, for him, can a soul be disordered and still be a single soul? A disordered soul would presumably be one in which spirit or appetite, or both, do not function as reason thinks they should. But if spirit or appetite are as singly aimed as Plato says, being unrestrained, they should pull us apart or go their own way alone. This, though, is something they do not do, and the only explanation for their not doing so is that they can dominate us too. Our whole souls can be mainly appetitive or mainly spirited, and in either case the rest of us is not left aside but is subordinate in a soul which is not ordered in the way in which Plato most approved. To say, therefore, that the reason alone can order a soul and also that there are disordered souls is to have inconsistent claims.

It is not even sound or safe to retreat to say that, really, reason always orders us but that in a disordered soul it does not have full grip upon our spirit or appetite. Were that the case, spirit and appetite would still shear us apart or leave us smaller than we were; so much, then, for the struggle for proper ordering. Then too, such an explanation would leave as still unexplained who it is who has the ingenious but limited reason which struggles so for mastery. Is there a soul which *has* reason, spirit and appetite? Or is the soul the same as reason, spirit and appetite, somehow joined? On either option, there has to be some unity, some way of being together other than the way which reason alone provides. We therefore cannot stay with the claim that reason or the Good provides for our only unity.

But even if it is acknowledged that there are unities for things other than the Good, there may still, unreasonably, in last resort, be this excessive claim: that the unity which the Good provides is the best or finest unity there could be. There is no reasonable way, however, to support this claim. Allow that the unity which reason provides for things is not their only unity, and the primacy of reason cannot be argued on the ground that reason alone constitutes the being of a world. Allow that other realities provide for unities as comprehensive as the Good, and comprehensiveness is not an argument for primacy. What good argument remains? There seems to be none, nor can it merely stand to reason that what reason does is best. This is the very point in argument and there is no further standard to which we can appeal. Reason provides unities of a distinctive sort for things. But then practice, art and religion are ways of bringing things together too—and bringing them no less together than they are brought together by the Good. Granted, they are different ways. But they are not better or worse because of that, nor are they even then together without intelligence. A consistent Plato should therefore say that perfected reason provides a proper place for spirit and appetite, and that perfected spirit and appetite provide perfectly well, though in different ways, for reason too.

The Good, in the sketch of it which has been drawn here, is one reality and not the whole of things. Every other sort of reality touches it and is qualified by it in turn. We are ourselves qualified by it. In us, the Good is called *our nature.* The "our" stands for that in us which is affected by the Good, and the word "nature" means the distinctiveness in our being together with other individuals, with God, time, and, in its double role, the Good itself. These other realities also provide for ways in which things can be together. There is, for example, providence, history and community. The Good is not the only way in which things stand in connectedness. There must be other ways, otherwise the Good could not have its double role or provide its special unity. It is a final irrationality to think that, because we can know about everything, the principle through which we know about it is the only principle on which it is unified. The sounder view is that there is a single principle on which the *what* of things is known, but that there are other ways in which things make up a whole and through which we can get at them.

Profoundly reflective men come to feel that knowledge is but one access to the world. To enrich the access or to provide a supplement for it, Plato, for example, wants the philosopher to go back into the cave; Aristotle says that the widest life for men, not being gods, is in the state and politics; Kant thinks that reason can and should be practical; Hegel supposes that purest rationality will objectify itself; Marx challenges the philosophers who have hitherto tried only to understand the world to give themselves to changing it; and the great pragmatists think that the fullness for abstractions is found in practical activity. These are, of course, very different views. Yet they all testify to a narrowness in a kind of knowing, even if they do not diagnose it properly. The mistake in most of these accounts is in supposing that where knowing seems to be limited, its supplement will be knowing more. The mistaken idea is that knowing is the *only* way to get at everything. A better diagnosis of the limitation in knowledge is that, knowing is but one way, not the only way, of getting at the whole of things. It is not an incomplete way, not a partial way, it is not in any sense inadequate. The limitation one comes to feel is misconstrued in the idea that there must be more or other kinds of knowing. It is better to say that we know that, besides knowing, there are other ways of dealing with the world.

Knowing testifies at last to its being distinctively knowing. Not every way of getting at the world is knowing it. Knowing itself drives us from this mistake, when we see the contradictions it leads us to. The soundest view seems to be that knowing deals with everything, but that there are also other ways of dealing with the whole of things, that while one can live fully in knowing things, the life of reason is not the only life that men can have. All that can and should be done cannot be done only in knowing things. Still, while there are different kinds of lives, and equally full ones, no kind is better than the life of reason. Construed properly, the life of reason is not subordinate to any other kind of life. Nor are other kinds subordinate to it. It is not an attenuated version of other kinds of lives nor are they degenerate forms of it. The unreasonable demand that reason shall have dominion over everything has at last to be set aside. Then, the proper demeanor of the life of reason can be made out.

THE LIFE OF REASON

Singular occasions can testify to the kinds of lives we have. A man's colleagues may give him a watch when he retires, or someone may thank him or shake his hand. These are single events, linked and added onto others in his life. Though single, they nevertheless can signal and celebrate who he is and all that he has done. No kind of life has as its purpose merely to bring about some distant single state of things; no one works merely for a watch. One may, however, aim to make for himself the kind of life which others can one day celebrate in a fitting ceremonial. The kind of life one has, what makes it a kind of life, is active in all the events or parts of it. A life can have a consummation; there can be an event in it which shows most clearly what it is. But it is the whole of life and what makes for its being whole which defines what kind of men we are.

A life of reason is a whole and single life because there is a single principle in it. The struggle of a man of reason is to have the principle be manifest, more embracing, steady and secure. The principle is that everything is dealt with through the access to it which the Good provides. Men of reason, then, can deal with what is here and now, with the future, the divine and with the Good itself, with everything, and in a distinctive way. They can eat and sleep, make love, work and loaf, and tend even toward irrationalities, though all they do takes on the guise of reasoning. They have a kind of life, a life of reason. This kind of life is described by Santayana as "the unity given to all existence by a mind in love with the Good." How should this life, this unity, be understood?

The life of reason is a piece of reasoning writ large. It has the unity, the kind of unity, which is found in reasoning. To see just what it is, we can look to reasoning and then enlarge on what we see.

What is reasoning? It is a bringing together of ideas or representations; we bring them together into new knowledge. But not only that. For the ideas are combined so as to show why it is, or how it is, that what we come to claim is so. We conclude something in reasoning, and what we conclude is reached through having a reason for believing that what we conclude is true. We do not conclude something and only then search for a reason for thinking it is true. Concluding through a reason, or bringing something forward as a reason, or going through a reason to what we at last conclude, is the distinctive process of reasoning.

We miss seeing the unity of the process of reasoning if, mistakenly, we think that we move in reasoning from place to place, as if ideas were set out in a line and we looked at one of them and then another. We also miss it if we think that we move in reasoning from belief to belief. In reasoning, we come to form beliefs, but both the *what* of what we believe and our credence in it are shaped in the course of reasoning.

The *what* of what we conclude comes from the beliefs with which we start. For all our ignorance and uncertainty at the start of reasoning, we start with and from beliefs. They are ample enough to lead to what we want to know and our credence in them extends to what we at last conclude. It is no coincidence that we always have beliefs enough to remove our ignorance and to acquire the new beliefs we need. The reason for this is that our specific ignorance is made specific through what we already know. We do not find ourselves in ignorance and then have to ask whether we know anything which will remove or reduce the ignorance—as if we might not know enough and have the ignorance be irremovable. We would not suffer this or that specific ignorance unless we already knew enough to have it set aside. The specific ignorance of a child depends on the knowledge of the child; the ignorance of the philosopher, on what he already claims to know.

Our move in reasoning, therefore, is not merely an adding of one item to a list of items because we see that it is implicated in the items which we have already thought or written down. Rather, feeling for what it is we want to know, we are already thinking of things we had earlier known, and these in turn, out of the urgency of our ignorance, are shaped to yield what sets the urgency of ignorance to rest. Ignorance stirs beliefs to prominence; they reach into and fill out what we do not know, substance and credence at once. Reasoning is, therefore, circular or spiral, with meanings in it changing all the time. There is nothing straight-lined in it at all. A good question, as the saying goes, is already more than half answered. It shows us what will answer it. The seeming paradox in ignorance is that when we know just what it is we do not know, our ignorance, awaiting only readjustments, is already gone. To reason, to make clear what we do not know, is to bring our knowledge to still greater clarity. Whether we think of ignorance as a darkness or a gap, the knowledge which makes it possible is ample enough to light or fill it up. The process of lighting or filling is continuous; there are no breaks in it.

Are there breaks, however, between pieces of reasoning? For many purposes, it is helpful to think that there are, that there are bounded stretches of reasoning which are preceded and followed by something which is not itself reasoning. We also talk of a beginning of a piece of reasoning and of an end to it, as if the reasoning is what goes on in between. But apart from special purposes and familiar talk it is not strictly accurate to suppose that reasoning comes in pieces. We can begin to see the continuity between "pieces of reasoning" by seeing that their so-called beginnings and endings are not finally marked out: close inspection shows that they are in fact parts of a wider whole of reasoning.

Look first at the start of a piece of reasoning. Where does it begin? What does it start from? The usual answers are that we begin because of a doubt or a question. What causes us to start a piece of reasoning is, however, not itself our start; it only leads us to make a start. How, then, should the spread between the provocation and the start be understood? Is it filled with reasoning or not? If reasoning is an activity, if it is something we can undertake deliberately, then, after the provocation, there should be deliberation about whether we will cause or allow reasoning to occur or not. We can hardly be blamed for not reasoning if there could not be good reasons for undertaking a course of thought. Where questions are complicated and there have to be economies, there is, as we know, a good deal of thought about whether a course of reasoning or investigation should be started or not. In all cases, however, there *must* be some thought on this point; for the space between the provocation and the start of reasoning cannot be a blank. We have to move from a provocation to a start, but it is reasoning itself that takes us through this course. For one thing to be a provocation and for something else to be a start in reasoning, there has to be still more reasoning. We have to conclude that something is a provocation and that a start in reasoning will best be made from certain premises. The start of a so-called piece of reasoning occurs inside of wider thought.

Reasoning also spreads beyond what we usually take to be the end of a piece of reasoning. It does this because no single so-called piece of reasoning ever fully satisfies its own intent. The common observation that one question leads to another suggests why this is so: one question can lead to another only if the concern which leads us to the reasoning that answers our first question is not entirely satisfied in it. One question would not otherwise lead to another; the occurrence of subsequent questions would be a coincidence. The concern whose challenge leads us into a piece of reasoning can, therefore, lead us to still further reasoning. We come from the first, ready for another and still others, and all these reasonings stand together as a whole.

But concluding a piece of reasoning is more than merely being ready for further reasoning. Strictly, even on the view that there are discrete pieces of reasoning, a conclusion leads us into or is itself another piece of reasoning. The argument for this point works this way: the conclusion of a piece of reasoning is a part in that piece of reasoning. Yet we also want to detach the conclusion from the reasoning itself; we want to use it by itself, apart from the beliefs which led to it. Initially, we wanted a conclusion which would remove our doubt and ignorance and solve our problem. But we wanted it not for that alone. We wanted something we could use in the course of whatever it was that we were doing before we were provoked to special thought. At the close of a piece of reasoning, we have got what we need. We therefore move from saying (1) that we conclude that this is so to saying (2) that having concluded that this is so, we can *therefore* now undertake afresh what we some time ago proposed. What is most often called a conclusion is neither wholly in nor wholly outside of what is usually marked off as a piece of reasoning. Were it confined in the reasoning, we could do nothing with it. Were it wholly outside, it would be an item which did not testify to its having a warrant, to its being an achievement of rationality. In strictness, a conclusion would best be regarded as consummating a piece of reasoning which is itself subordinate in a reasoning which is of even wider, longer reach.

Neither the start nor the end of a piece of reasoning is a sharp boundary, beyond which there is a blank in which there is no reasoning, no thought of any kind. Rather, reasoning melds with reasoning. Portions that we remember or can reconstruct may for good reasons be isolated for examination; they are the portions in which we are most controlled, deliberate, least consciously habituated. They may even be the most important parts and crucial turns of thought. It would be a wrong picture of our minds, however, to think of us as mainly blank, as now and then vibrant with feeling or perception, and then occasionally occupied in a chain or spread or train of thought. It would be better to think of us as always reasoning, though perhaps only now and then attentive in our thought. Instead of saying that thought occurs in us, it is better to say, as Peirce suggested, that we are in thought, even if we are not much occupied with the fact of being there. Reasoning, more or less controlled, more or less heightened, spreads through the whole of life.

This claim, that reasoning is spread through the whole of our lives, is not the stronger claim that lives can consist of reasoning. All of us have minds, but not all of us live a life of reason. The life of a man of reason is a piece of reasoning. Other men, with other kinds of lives, reason all the time. But their lives are not the same as reasoning. What is the difference? The difference is that our aim in a life of reason brings everything into our lives as items in our reasoning; everything is acknowledged as a portion in a reasoning which, thereby, is the entirety of a life; it is simply a life in which reasoning is writ large. Other sorts of men unify their lives in a different way. They reason, but they are not aimed so as to be a piece of reasoning.

The structure and the content in a life of reason are the same as those in reasoning itself. Items are significant; each is in the nature of a sign, and the activity of the life is the discerning and developing of the meaning of the signs. Everything in a life of reason is experienced as a sign; and everything is interpreted as showing how the Good bears on it. How is it, though, that things become signs for us? How do they signify the Good? How is their rational meaning developed? And how full is the life in which this development takes place? These are the questions we have to answer now.

There are many ways of representing things. The idea that there is but a single way has led us to distort the significance which is found in art and in religion, as we will see. Still, there is a basic structure in all representation, no matter the form it takes specifically. It is that whatever is significant is part of, or derived from, or an instance of some other sort of thing. As we see this partiality in a thing, we see the thing as a sign, either of the thing it partializes or of something else which is or might be part of that same more comprehensive entity.

The inescapability of this structure has become especially evident in modern thought. In Descartes, for example, it is explained in a doctrine of formal and objective reality, in the notion that in the light of nature items attest to us their significance. It also occurs in Descartes' observation that it is only as we see ourselves to be dependent on God that we understand that we are images, representations of God himself. For Kant, categories account for the fact that sensuosities, in themselves meaningless, signify possible contents of categorially organized experience. For Peirce, laws and regularities explain how present items are portents of what is to come. Nowadays, the talk is of rules or uses of language, even conventions of speech; what counts as an item of speech and as the meaning of such an item depends upon those rules. There are still other castings of the structure. In one form or another, it is unavoidable. What form is most likely to be best?

We can answer this question if, again, we talk about the Good and its double role in knowing things. It is as we bring these roles together that we come both (1) to represent things to ourselves and (2) to be changed as we understand what we have made them mean. The Good is the covering entity which enables us to construe other things as rationally significant. To have them be significant, we have to go through them toward the Good and through the Good toward them. The Good in both these routes is the middle term in the inference in which the meanings are discerned and developed and in which we ourselves, as those who mean and understand, are changed. This will perhaps become clearer by our comparing the development of meaning and of mind to the famous and familiar journey of the philosopher in Plato's image of the cave. The image shows us that we have to go away from, and then come back to, what we want to understand.

In Plato's image, as long as we are chained within the cave, we do not really know what is going on. We are not entirely in the dark, though, for something, not much, can be discerned. Really to know what is within the cave, we have to escape the cave entirely. The Good itself is to be seen. Then, when we go back into the cave, because of what we have seen outside, we can make out the shape of the shadows and the sounds.

This image, or something in it, is surely right, and there have been reflections on its rightness into modern times. If really we are to know, we must see the Good itself, possess it as it is alone. It is perhaps the same to claim that a suitably reflective man will have hold upon truths of reason, categories, or *a priori* truths. We have to move toward the Good from the cave. But we have also to move from the Good back into it. Seeing the Good alone is not knowing all that can be known. There are, then, these two routes: toward the Good and toward other realities through it. We have to take them both. Plato's ingenious image shows us the Good in this double role. The only trouble in Plato's view is that the Good for him is so complete that it cannot play this double role. It is not itself a sign, nor does it give us a sign that it can qualify other realities or be qualified by them in turn. Only if this is true of the Good can there be routes both toward and away from it; only in a different Good can the routes be conjoined as our knowledge of the world. For Plato, the Good seems to bear upon the world through specific forms, perhaps one should say forms more specific than the Good. But since even these are all complete, their bearing is not plain; it is not even possible. To change the image, then, we have to say that the Good is not so complete or self-enclosed as Plato claims. We do not see it or have it entirely alone; we do not even see the sun that way. Plato's image is indeed sounder than his formulated view. It shows the sun as casting light upon other things. This is what the doctrine should also show: that the Good itself testifies to there being other sorts of things and they, in turn, show in themselves a mark of it. Only with this sort of Good will knowing be by reasoning, and only then will reasoning have a middle term.

Now, apart from Plato's image, the point is that items come to be meaningful, to be signs or representations, only as they are seen to be derived from, to specify, or to be qualified by another sort of thing, and that they are seen to be this way only as we can also see them through the thing they qualify. Something is a word, for example, as we see it as an instance of a rule, but we can see it as an instance of a rule only if the rule itself shows us that there can be items in which the rule is found. All that is significant is acknowledged in this twofold way, and the varieties, the kinds of significance, depend upon the sort of items that are specified or qualified. They also depend on the way in general in which we are concerned.

A man of reason is concerned to deal with the whole of things through knowing them. This concern of his leads him into each of his inferences and, as unfulfilled in any one of them, it readies him to reason more. It is as though he were the Good itself seeking to find itself or to insinuate itself into the course of things. A man, however, is not the Good; he is only qualified by it. He therefore confronts, opposes and undergoes other realities. For him, these are items to be understood; they are, as it were, his minor premises. Since each of these is itself touched by the Good, each is understandable. To understand them in fact, though, we cannot simply stay with them alone, trying to penetrate them through, as if their intelligible nature were closed inside of them. We have to bring and hold together (1) what we discern of things through the Good, and (2) what we discern of the Good through them. *A this somewhat* together with *a somewhat as the Good* is a representation of the *this* we want to know and of the *what* which we understand. Holding together an access to the Good through a thing and through the Good to it is having it in terms of the Good at which reason aims. This is what a man of reason is concerned to do. In doing it, he is an inference, a knowing mind, and, as we will also see, he is himself a sign.

The Good makes every sort of thing understandable. It is the embracing context within which, so far as it is intelligible, everything is *what* it is. For men of reason, every thing is a sign of the Good, and their lives are richer and more ample as there is more that they understand, or more that they clearly see. Though they are attentive to all sorts of things, one more than another will plainly show the Good and, then, naturally men of reason will be more preoccupied with it. It will be for them a higher thing, something lofty; denser, lower things will not have so large a place within their lives. Everything that is experienced, however, is for them the question: what is shown here of the Good? Sometimes the answer is so familiar or we are so inattentive that the question is only barely formed. At other times, with items which seem especially luminous or promising, the question stirs afresh our wonder, the whole passion to know the truth and everything. No matter our passion, though, we succeed finally in knowing very little. But it is not this disappointment alone which torments those of us who most want to live through thought. The twin role of the Good in knowing also causes a tearing tension which men of reason never overcome.

They are to go through the Good toward the things they know and through the to-be-known toward the Good itself; they are to hold the two together. The balance is delicate, and for many men there is an ambiguity about which route shall be most prominent. Shall we be pulled by the things, the minor premisses? Should we stay mainly with the Good itself?

Many a man of reason occupies himself with signs of the Good; he mixes with the world and tries to have it show him the Good it means. The sound accent in the otherwise overstated claim that reason shall have dominion over things is that everything is or can be seen to be rationally significant. Out of arrogant error, feeling that he has lucid grasp of the Good, or out of a fearful unsureness that he does not have it yet, many a man of reason turns to what is about him now. It is either a place where he can better make out the Good, or it is a refuge from the Good's austerity and its demands. No man can live in and with the Good alone. He also has to deal with other sorts of things, and he deals with them well or not. He is excellent or not as he brings to them a clear vision and a supple hold upon the Good. This is very hard to do (even if his reasons and motives for emphasizing minor premises are sound), which is why so many experts and other knowledgeable men have so little sense. They lose their way; for them it is not lit well enough by the Good. Too quickly, they are caught in routine ways of knowing and understanding things.

One can, however, go too far the other way—to accent the Good and to try to get at it and neglect what is about us now. This is the philosophical figure of the caricature, the man who falls into a deep hole while looking at the stars. He knows the sense of everything, or he tries at knowing it, but then he neither searches for nor sees that sense in anything specifically. He is abstracted; his mind is absented from the world, and all he knows of it, if he is asked, is bare and empty platitude.

Concerned for the whole of things through that access to it provided by the Good, what the man of reason most needs for excellence is a balanced hold on his routes to and from the Good. There is no rule by which it can be found. Finding it is indeed knowing when and where and how, as special cases of the Good, rules are themselves to be applied. Nor can anyone put him at the balance point by instruction, training or advice. Each has to find it for himself; he has to think for himself and, continually, to locate himself, to adjust himself, in connection both with the Good and what he comes to know. No man of reason always does this well. Still, it is only as he has proportioned hold on the routes to and from the Good that he has knowledge at its best. Only then does his own meaning become clear and understandable.

The man of reason is not always understood. He is often

criticized, not because he wants to know but because in knowing, something vital seems to get dried out of him. The complaint is that there is no joy in him, that he does not feel enough, or that he deals with things improperly, that he does not acknowledge them for what they are but takes them only as signs of something else. Still another and an old complaint is that he has no piety. These complaints can all be sound. They are sound, however, only against men of reason who are not as reasonable as they might be. They are not sound in general.

What is the right measure of joy, propriety and humility? How much joy, how much feeling is enough? Dally in, live in, be overridden in the immediacies of a moment, and one neglects whatever else there is and will not know a thing, or very little anyway. Fail to see what things are significant, and one fails to see what they are and then can only treat them improperly. Neglect to know that there is a meaning even to God, and one could not even testify in faith. Men of reason may well fail in being excellent as men of thought. But it would be impractical, tasteless, impious and, of course, an error to claim that they should be different kinds of men. As excellent in being the kind of men they are, as holding in balance their routes to what there is, they can be understood. That in fact is exactly the way they are most appropriately to be dealt with: as men who are to be understood as signs of the Good, or as one might also say, as teachers. Perhaps, however, only other men of reason can deal with them that way.

An excellent man of reason is a knower through and through, not in his head alone. All and everything he does is a knowing; he thinks in his body, in his walk and look and touch, and even in his passivity. He is an incarnation of the Good. How he is such an incarnation—this is what he teaches others, and this is what they can learn because of him. Not many teachers in the schools are men of thought, nor do they teach us much. Fortunately, some are vital in the concern to know, and what they have to teach is very plain: it is what it is to be a man of thought. There is nothing more important they can teach. The way to teach it, we learned long ago from Socrates. He asked whether virtue can be taught; his own life showed us how it could. It was a mistake for him to think that all of us are fundamentally men of thought. But those who are can teach virtue by making a life in which thought is excellent and its excellence is made plain. For Socrates, this was a life of talk, or dialogue, of the questioning and answering in which young men came to see who they are.

A Socratic dialogue is the world in small, though it is large enough to test who young men are. Socrates shapes and controls its temptations and rewards, and he sees that jeopardies are not overpowering. He provokes the men who live in it to think on their own. And in the course of doing this, he says whatever he has to say to vitalize their concern, to quiet their pretense, to bolster their courage and to keep them from irrelevance. His greatest trial is to keep young men from repeating, without understanding, what others have already claimed. It is no defect in a knower, of course, to agree with what others say. But one has to think for himself before he can agree with someone else. The young men with whom Socrates talks, young men at any time, repeat what they have heard, or, in irritation, they deny it, without in either case really understanding what they claim. In the repetition, in the denials, they steady and locate themselves. Without destroying their place or what steadies them, Socrates has to set them on their own, to touch them without scarring or stopping them. He knows that they already think; so he creates a balanced situation in which they can think still more, or an unbalanced one, to mark the unbalance he finds in them. He does this with words, or rather, with himself. The words are intrusive devices which provoke a perceptive student to see what Socrates stands for or represents.

All men of reason, like Socrates, testify to the Good they incorporate. Socrates was a paradigm of this incarnation. A poor and ugly man, untalented in an artistic craft, irritated by an understandably shrewish wife, and without colleagues of his own stature and concern, he nevertheless stayed steady in his aim and avoided even that last vanity of wise men, the idea that their wisdom can be told. His teaching was itself a search for a firmer knowing, for a firmer hold upon the Good. All who teach need students to slow them from their foolishness. They have to hold in themselves an access to and from the Good. They are themselves this join, and they are not pettily to intrude on it or to obscure or overshadow it. Those who succeed in this are at once remarkably anonymous —who, we ask, was the real Socrates?—and also large and full as individual men. They mean the Good, they know it, and as holding both accesses together they do the Good they know. They show it forth. But this is something that not everyone, not every sort of man, will understand.

Chapter IV

The Life in Art

———

Like men of practice and of reason, those who live in art take some account of everything. They too deal with the whole of things, though their way of doing it is different from the ways of other kinds of men. Of all the realities, time is the one to which men of art are most sensitive. Through it, they aim at all the rest. Just as practice and reason reach into everything through the access to it which a basic reality provides, lives in art place one reality in prominence. Then too, as other men will also do, those who live in art try to have everything enhanced by what is for them the nodal point in things. Time shows itself most plainly in the immediacies of our experience, in the sensuous, in the becoming and the fleetingness of the present moment. No other sorts of men make it central in their lives. Because they do not, they judge that art dallies in sheer fiction and they accuse it of delicate impracticality. The judgment and accusation are biased and unwarranted. Nevertheless, they reveal something of the distinctiveness of the life in art.

Take first the charge made by men of reason that works of art are fictions. This acknowledges that the works are representative, but then the question is what a fiction represents. Does it represent something real or not? The options are thought to be extreme, and untenable, for a fiction cannot represent something that is not real—there are no unrealities. On the other hand, if a fiction represents the real, it does so either truly or not, and there is no other way of representing things. What makes something a fiction, then, is either *what* is represented or a special *way* of representing things. Neither claim—this is the charge —can be made out and, therefore, there really are no fictions after all. Since this argument is important, let me go over the alternatives again. One claim is that it is too extreme to say that a fiction represents something, but that what it shows us is in no sense real. Were a work to represent nothing real, the unreal thing it sets before us would have been made in the very making of the work and be a part of it. The artist would be a minor god who cannot set the fiction he creates apart from the work which carries it. No one, however, or almost no one, credits artists with this magical creativity. The narrowly reasonable view of a fiction, the other option, is that a fiction is a falsity, that artists do not see the real aright, but that they can make a work of art so ingeniously that its falsity can seem to be a truth. A modern version of this discerning but unsound view is that art is made of metaphors. The critical upshot of the alternatives, then, is that those who live in art are really men of reason; only, there is little reason in them and they are distracted by sensuosities. They are not reasonable enough rightly to discern the world.

The most famous critical appraisal of art given by a man of reason was given by Plato in *The Republic*. More than most philosophers, more even than many artists, Plato understood the power of the arts. He saw that art readily moves men to action. This is why he believed it to be so serious a challenge to philosophy and to the rule which, he thinks, philosophy should have. The challenge is about ideas, and about the place they are to have in the ordering of our souls. Both artists and philosophers, according to Plato, deal with ideas. But philosophy tries to have us understand them and art does not. Artists use ideas only to inform the sensuosities in which most of us delight. The ideas then become effective in us, but we don't understand them, nor do we, through the arts, come to know how or when or why they are properly to be used. The artist himself does not understand his own ideas; he doesn't fashion his works so that their effects have the proper place in us. He knows by inspiration, in a kind of madness; his creating has no thorough rationale. The right role of art, according to Plato, is to promote the preeminence of rationality—but then, once that end is achieved, once a stable ordering of our souls is reached, art has no further use. We are to deal with ideas, with the ideas themselves, apart from their being incorporated in anything. Excellent works of art are instrumental. They help us become more reasonable. They are of help, however, only to those who are not philosophers, or not yet philosophers. Philosophers themselves do not dally with the arts. Plato thinks that there is not enough in them for us to know.

Plato's judgment of the inspired artist depends on his view that there is a pre-eminent reality and that it is seen for what it is only through the use of mind. For Plato, this reality is the Good, and sensuosities, transience, becoming—these obscure our grasp of it. In the finest use of reason, we have nothing to do with art or with any other representations. We deal with the Good itself, and by itself. Were it sound to claim that Plato's Good is the most basic of things, then Plato's view of the power and degeneracy of art would be sure and inescapable. Those who live in art would be lesser knowers. Their lives would not be focused as they should be.

Were there, however, to be other realities as basic as the Good, were art to deal with everything through one of them, then art would have an equal place with rationality. This is the claim which is central in this essay: that there is a reality as basic and as embracing as the Good, and that art deals with everything through it. On this view, the concern of art and the concern of reason are not the same, though they are comparable in reach and shape. Since they are distinct, it is a mistake to describe those who live in art as knowers. It is defensive even to say that their sensitivity is a knowing of a special kind. One neither sees nor serves art well in claiming that its excellence is intellectual. But while distinct from knowledge, art can nevertheless be understood to represent the real. A fiction is a special way of incorporating and setting out what is really there. This view of a fiction lets us see the soundness in Plato's view that the ideas in works of art are near to being trivial and that they are not commended through the works as being sound. It can do this, however, without stain to art's integrity. We need only see that the reality through which reason aims is subordinate in art's equally basic but distinct concern.

A second revealing judgment or accusation of the arts is that art is not a separate enterprise but a species of practice: it is a delicate practicality; an artist is a practical man without strong force or effectiveness. His lesser practice is on those areas in our experience which are effete and not urgent. Just as it is easy to confuse those who live in art with imperfect men of reason, we can also mistake an artist's creative activity with the mastery and control of things at which we aim in practice. Both artists and practical men are makers of things, and between works of craft and works of art it may seem that the only differences are in degree. Both (1) in their constructive making and (2) in the ways in which the works are taken up, craft and art can seem too similar to be entirely distinct activities.

The issues which show that there is a distinction in kind between art and practice are especially controversial. An extended discussion of them is needed, supported by illustrative, incidental points. Perhaps it will be best to start by examining our responsiveness to act. Here, what we will finally have to claim is that only those who live in art take up art as art and that, as artists say, the rest of us are philistines. Then we can go on to the obvious but reasoned view that works of art are made by artists, that the concern which defines the artist as a kind of man also defines his creating and the works he makes.

To begin, then, with our responsiveness: works of art are usually set before us as being works of art. We are introduced to them as works of art in museums, galleries, theaters, studios and stores. By the ways in which they are made available to us, we are readied to treat them as being art; these ways are signs to us that we will be confronting artistic works. But despite the signs and preparations, not all of us respond to art as art, as those who live in art can do. The reason for this is simply that our dealings with things are always shaped by the concerns which define the kinds of men we are. We can never cease to be a kind of man, nor can we change the kind we are. As a consequence, not all of us can deal with art as art.

Men of reason, for example, can deal with art only within whatever latitude their concern for knowledge will allow. This is true of other sorts of men as well. The leading concern of men who do not live in art may at times be relaxed in them and then, perhaps, they can be more responsive to art. Even then, however, art comes to them as qualified by their concerns, never quite as art. It is a species of practice, reason or religiosity. Excellent men of practice, reason and faith may sense that art can be approached with a concern different from their own. But since such a concern is not their own, they never quite deal with art as do the men whose lives are aimed with it. For men of practice, art should always have moving effectiveness; for men of reason, it should give us knowledge, and a religious man asks that it support his faith. Only those whose concern it is to have a life in art can stand apart from these demands. Such men, as we will see, deal with everything as a kind of art.

The judgment that only certain men have a sense of art as art may seem unduly harsh and too severe. It is a demanding view. But, then, it sees that art is itself demanding and that we do not respond to it fully when we respond to it casually or only occasionally, when there is a respite in our otherwise earnest lives. Art is difficult. Its fullest appreciation is accessible only to those who are tuned to and trained for it. Others of us never get into it as those who live in art can do, with the fullest of proprieties. Still—and this second point may soften the seeming harshness of the judgment some—those of us who are not men of art can accommodate a great deal of art, even if we do not deal with it on its own terms. It cannot matter much that we do not deal with it as such if we can in other ways take large account of it. The special concerns through which we deal with everything will also encompass art, and with some feel as well for the values which are really to be found in it. Men of practice, reason and faith need not distort the arts beyond all recognition when they take account of them. Besides, there are men who work especially to show those of us who are not in art, how, within the scope of our own concerns, we can best take hold of it. These are the critics. They can make sense of art, or they can make it effective in and enhancing for our lives.

Ideally, there should be four sorts of critics, one each for the different kinds of men. There should be critics who help men of practice, reason and faith to find out how, within their own concerns, they can make an amply appreciative place for art. Apart from teachers of art or artists who apprentice younger artists to themselves, there should also be critics who help men of art to be more disciplined and discerning about the very arts with which they are concerned. In fact, however, we seem not to have this variety of critics. The criticism of the present day is mainly limited in kind.

We do not even have good practical critics. The reviewers who publish in the large public press are not critics but journalists. They tell us about performances of the arts—usually whether these performances are worth the price or not. They are often effective in getting us to come to performances or in keeping us away from them. But they hardly help us to get into the arts themselves.

The critics who teach the arts in the schools and colleges are often more helpful. Most of their instruction, however, is planned as if all their students were diminutive men of reason—they are taught what there is to know about the arts and what the arts themselves are supposed to help us know. As it happens, then, those students whose turn is practical or religious are hardly touched by what these teachers do; nor are those whose bent is toward knowledge long satisfied with what they come to think is retrograde and idiosyncratic philosophy. Mainly, and unfortunately, our teachers fail to have us place the arts within our lives.

Why is instructed criticism now on such a narrow path? There have been many explanations; there may be many partial causes for the fact. Not the least of them, it seems, is that the arts are taught in the colleges where those who teach them are often intimidated by colleagues whose concern is genuinely with reason, with finding and knowing the truth. Professors of the arts then feel that they too must have something to profess; it will not do *merely* to help students read and write and see and hear. So instruction turns to history and themes, to philological items, or to one or another sort of analysis justified by one or another sort of theory about what men really are and what they mean. Or, what is most often done, teachers turn the arts into a vast metaboly of images, metaphors and symbols through which, somehow, something important is supposed to be said. None of these means has made art vital to many of us, nor have they even much enhanced our tastes.

Were there more variety in the ways in which we are taught the arts, were they at times dealt with more unreasonably, were we in fact encouraged to try them, our hold upon them might be larger and more responsive than, for most of us, it is. But whatever the cause of the failures of our teachers, it is plain why their job is so hard. They have to show those of us who cannot finally deal with art as art how we can, amply and with least distortion, take the arts into ourselves. They try to show us how our concern can be likened to the concern through art, and they show us what we might then see. Or, so they should, and they should also show us how the arts, as incorporated in our own concerns, can enhance these concerns themselves. It does not demean the arts to see that they can support concerns other than the concern for art, to see their power, sense and spirit. Critics cannot make us men of art if we are natively of a different kind. They can do enough, however, or so they should, to take the harshness from the judgment that only those who live in art can deal with art as such. All of us can take some fine but practical, reasonable, or spiritual hold of art. Critics might show us how. It is a loss to us that they are not yet very versatile and that they address themselves to so small an audience.

Those who do not live in art, then, no matter how well practiced, instructed or charitable do not deal in art in the terms that art distinctively provides. There is for them, therefore, no firm, no final difference between a work of art and craft; nor is there, depending on the kinds of men they are, an essential difference between a work of art and a sign or exemplar of the truth or an idol or an offering. Whether something which is made is a work of art or not depends partly on how it is taken up; it depends on the place it has in the lives of those who deal with it. For those who live in art, the works are art, and much else is art as well. For those whose lives are of another kind, the work is a version of what they take everything to be. It is perhaps a particularly fine piece of craftsmanship, or a piece particularly revealing of the truth, or perhaps it is a special support for faith.

It does no good to object to this by insisting that, really, art should be dealt with as art. This is exactly what is being claimed. Every sort of thing should be dealt with as it is, and art is to be dealt with in this way too. But it is only for those who live in art that art is distinctive. For other men, the only way to deal with art is through their own concerns, and this is the right way to deal with it. Good art is just what these concerns show it to be: well made, revealing and supportive. It is no distortion of art to see that it can be appropriated in different ways, all of which are commensurate with what it is distinctively. We misunderstand art badly if we think that it cannot be dealt with appropriately in different ways. How little versatile, significant or important, art would be were this not the case.

A distinction between works of art and other works can, of course, be made. The distinction is connected with distinctions between the different kinds of men. It is not independent of those distinctions, nor is it the most fundamental one. The demand that there be a distinction between works of art and other sorts of works is an easy one to satisfy, only the distinction does not take us far. Those who press for it usually want it as preliminary to making the argument that because art is distinctive, we should all behave toward it in a specially appropriate way. The points here, by contrast, are simply (1) that artists are a distinctive kind of men, (2) that the works of artists are works of art, (3) that these works are, because of being art, available to men of other kinds in only certain ways, and (4) that in these ways there is room for large appreciation of the arts. Grant, as is argued here, that there is a distinction between artists and other kinds of men, and a distinction between art and craft is made accordingly. This last distinction, though, has no useful import of its own. It does not even help us much to see the very issues in terms of which it is made. We will see these issues better when we look to the special making which is the making of a work of art. This is the second of the matters which is to be discussed.

ART AND REALITY

Those who live in art aim at everything through one strand of reality. They also take this strand as a measure of the unity of all the rest. The reality through which artists deal with everything is what, in this essay, is called time. Time is not merely present-ness, passage, or transience; these, as was suggested earlier, are interplays between time and individuals. Nor is time even the present, or the past, or the future. These are divisions of time; they are parts of it, but not as it is alone. Although time is a single, basic reality, to say what it is, how it is, or even when it is, we have to refer to the other basic realities with which it is joined; we have to refer to individuals, and to the Good and God. Time is altogether with these other realities (1) in the ways in which these others provide a unity for all there is; these others, in turn, are together with time (2) in the distinctive way in which time embraces them.

This second feature of time is the one to which we have been most attentive in the West. It is the idea that time embraces everything, that everything is inside of it. The first idea has been formulated in the East. It is the notion that things affect time, or that they seem to affect it, their seeming individualities seem to scar its unitary nature with transience. Both themes are mainly sound. If they are modified a bit, both can be retained com-patibly. Together, they show that time is bound up with other realities in the different ways which those realities provide, and that, from its side, time also unifies all of these realities, pervading and embracing them. Time can thereby be a focus on everything there is, and through every other thing we can also move toward time. This two-sidedness—through and toward time's basic real-ity—helps to define a life in art. Can we understand its structure and see something of its content too?

Although our concern is without limit, we are localized beings and we can act only in certain ways. We have to deal with things as we are, from where we are, and we have as well to be responsive to the demands they make on us. Depending on the kinds of men we are, we deal with things in different ways and have different focused ends. Those who live in art see that while time is both congealed and bounded inside of individuals, it also suffuses them and they try to deal with things mainly to take account of this fact. The most passive way of dealing with things is to experience them, and in the life of art experiences are aesthetic. Let me try to say what aesthetic experiences are.

To experience things aesthetically is not to experience aesthetic things. Experience is not neutral and then defined as being of a kind because of the kind of thing experienced. Nor is an aesthetic experience an experience in which a certain kind of character is prominent, as if, again, experience were neutral and then said to be aesthetic because of a kind of character which occurs in it. Nor is an experience aesthetic because of the attitude we have in being open to experience, as if all that were then experienced were colored by the openness in which it is received. These doctrines, revealing as they are, are too conservative. They each suppose that experiencing is a neutral holding together of things and that experience is then classified by the kinds of things which are held together, or by the prominent effect of one of them, or by the intent we bring to the experience, or by the upshot of the experience. It will be stronger and sounder to take virtually the opposite view—to hold that our experiencing is always a holding together of things in a certain way, that an experience is ôf a kind because of its distinctive unity, and that because of the unity (1) the objects of the experience are said to be of a certain kind, (2) qualities of a certain kind are prominent, and (3) attitudes or intents of a certain sort occur. Unless this, or something like this, is so, art cannot be a basic concern. For aesthetic objects are not basic kinds of things; aesthetic qualities, if real, are only adventitious, and the so-called isolated aesthetic attitude is perverse. Define aesthetic experience by one or all of these features, and it is doubtful either that there are aesthetic experiences or doubtful that they are fundamental as to kind. If there is to be a kind of life in art, aesthetic experience must be a kind of experience, and the kind cannot be defined by an object or quality in the experience or even, as if there were such a thing, by the attitude we have as we enter into it.

For an experience to be one experience, it has to be an experience *by* one individual and an experience *of* something which is itself singular. It has also to be had *through* or *with* some single thing and to be consolidated or closed in *by* something singular. One experience is made up of ones. The words "of," and "by," "with" or "through," when we use them in describing an experience, mark the singularities which define the singleness of one experience. They mark the comprehensive unity of the experience and the subordinate unities of which the comprehensive one is made. Different sorts of experience provide for these unities in different ways; practical experience is unitary in a different sense than an experience of knowing. The first is, perhaps, an effecting; the second, a judging. Comparably, an aesthetic experience is distinctive as a kind of experience because of its distinctive unity. Its major, or formal unity, as we will see, is provided for by time: everything in the experience and we ourselves as having it are within the singular spread of time. This notion—comparable to Mrs. Langer's notion of the presentational—promises to give meaning to the idea that aesthetic experience is appreciative, and that it is full of feeling and value.

Each of us deals with time and is caught up in it. In part, we help to cause it to come to pass. This feature of our activity is prominent in practice, where along with other individuals, we individuate ourselves and last for a time. If I am not a practical man, however, my concern is not focused through the urgency of maintaining myself against the rush of time. I can deal with time so as to make another feature of it prominent, and if I live in art this is what I do. In a life in art, my concern is not to stand over and against other individuals; it is not to press for renewed, persistent individuality, nor to incorporate in myself an overwhelming time. Instead, it is to make prominent that spread of time which pervades me and my contemporaries, which unites me and my contemporaries, and which, in fact, is our being as together at a present time. The mark of our being individuals in a present is that we seize and grasp and resist and defend. But there is also then an extensiveness in which we are together and for which we do not fight; it is a space in which are now found the places delimited by our resistances. This extensiveness is part of our being. We never quite get time wholly inside our separate selves. Because we do not, we are together with others now; we are one with them and not distinguished from them. In a present, then, because of the ways in which we deal with time and because of the ways in which it enters through and into us, we are only partly distinct from other individuals. That spread of present time in which we are not individuated, that extensiveness of ourselves which is continuous with others now, is the singularity which makes for the unity in aesthetic experiences. Those who live in art try to make this feature of time, this feature of themselves, prominent in experience. And aesthetic objects, or excellent ones, are those contemporaries of ours which we can experience in such a way that the singularity of time is the most pervasive and unifying aspect of the experience.

To bring out again the feature of temporality which is so important in art, we should see that as time is and comes into a present, it is not thoroughly fractured into portions which are then our private temporalities. Nor does time as a whole stand entirely aside from us, as if we were non-temporal, inactive beings who happen to be located inside of it. Time is a single entity which moves into and through us, but such hold as we each separately take of it does not set us off altogether from our contemporaries. We are and remain continuous with them in a suffusing time, and the togetherness we have with them which is owed to time provides for the unity characteristic of an aesthetic experience. We can have no account of an aesthetic experience if we think that, first, we stand isolated and self-enclosed and that then, in some strange way, we experience other things by going beyond ourselves to take account of them. Nor are we helped by the idea that the things we take account of in experience produce effects inside our insulated selves which we then read as being signs of them. In aesthetic experience, there is no such insulation, no such separation from other things. Such distinction and division as occur between items in aesthetic experience are inside of the experience itself, and they are unified in the experience by a pervasive time.

What is unified in an aesthetic experience is a variety of content. This variety is owed to the individuals who both border and enter the experience; it is a variety of sensuosities. Even though time stays whole and singular as it moves through us, its singularity is always toned by us. The urgent time which moves through us all is not discontinuous with the hold we have on it, with our own and individual presentness. Again, we are at once individual and distinct from others now, but we are also contemporaries of one another. It is the hold which we and the things which we experience have on the singular passing time which makes for the variety, the sensuosities, of our experience. Sensuosities are beings wholly of the present. As those who struggle with them in accounts of knowledge know, they are neither ours exclusively nor are they entirely in other things. They are a stuff of both our experience and of the things which we experience, the stuff which is the continuity of individuals with their common temporality. As we also know, variety in the sensuous can enhance and deepen an experience, or it can jeopardize its unity. Some aesthetic experiences are not intense. In others, the unity does not suffuse the contents through and through; there is too much sheer medley to the feeling; it is too unorganized.

A unifying form together with a variety of contents are not enough, however, to account for the unity of any kind of experience. Kant made this point plain when he talked, not only of the categories, but also of the schema and the other forms which are part of our experience of knowing things. Comparably, in aesthetic experience there must also be something which provides for a subordinate unity, and we have as well to take account of what it is in things which allows for there being a closure for experience.

The Good and God are the realities through which this fullness of an aesthetic experience is to be understood; these realities also enter into such experience. Had they no relevance to it, art would not take account of everything. There could also be no ground for supposing that in art there is a knowing of something, even if only a degenerate knowing, and there could be no threat to or support for faith. How, in detail, these, and indeed time and individuals themselves, enter into aesthetic experience requires a fuller morphology of experience than is appropriate for our discussion now. The lines of that morphology, however, are perhaps already clear, at least for the most familiar sort of aesthetic experience. They show themselves in the following way.

The common time which suffuses contemporaries is, as it is filled with them, a spread of sensuosities. Individuals themselves, verging into presentness and opposed to and resisting one another, are, as we saw before, almost torn apart. The stability, the nature, the intelligible togetherness they have with others is the Good, of which all other individuals also take account. This was a claim of an earlier argument. The stabilizing Good is not a surface character of individuals; it would not make them intelligible if it were only that. Rather, the Good penetrates them and enters even into the individuals as sensuous and as not markedly discrete. This is close to Plato's claim that in the world the Forms are overrun and slurred in the sensuousness of passage. Plato seems to think that sensuosities are the Good as overrun by flux or unreality. But even if this view is, as it seems to be, not acceptable in its detail, it is right to say with Plato that the Good is caught up in passage and that there it is subordinate to something else. The Good enters into aesthetic experience in a subordinate way; it provides a subordinate intelligibility, or harmony; it is the fittingness of the differing sensuosities as together in an experience whose supervening unity is the time common to contemporary individuals.

Finally, to account for the singularity of individuals, for the ruptures and closures that help to define a single aesthetic experience, we have to refer to the singularity of God. Of all the realities, God enters least into an aesthetic experience of individual things. Still, there could be no such experience entirely apart from him. He provides the focus which enables individuals to disclose themselves to one another in a common time. The doctrine that works of art are properly offerings to God comes close to stating what seems to be the connection between God and art.

The import of these condensed abstractions is, in summary, that an aesthetic experience is a distinctive kind of experience, that what makes for the unity of such experience defines it as to kind, that in aesthetic experience there are sensuosities, and closures and disclosures of individuals though these themselves do not define the experience as to its kind; then too, as we think what an aesthetic experience is, we have to see it not as a superficial or trivial or delicately effete piece of preciousness, but as a way of dealing even with the Good and God, with all the kinds of things. It is a basic way of being with and experiencing the whole of what is real.

But these descriptions, however accurate, are weighted too one-sidedly. The appreciativeness in the aesthetic experience of individuals has been overemphasized. Those who live in art do experience in this way; and they turn the things that they experience and they turn themselves to have enriched experience. Because they do, everything for them is, as it were, a work of art; everything submits itself to be aesthetically experienced. Some of those who live in art, however, also work to produce objects which we are to experience aesthetically. They are artists and what they produce are works of art. To proportion an account of aesthetic experience, something of the artist's creativity should also be understood.

Those who live in art but who do not produce objects which are to be experienced aesthetically can be said to be artists in the making of acts of appreciation; they produce the acts, the places, the roles for the things which are experienced, not the things themselves. Artists produce works of art. Works of art are artificial individuals, and if they are good, an experience of them, in being appreciative, can also be (1) effective, and by being (2) meaningful, point beyond the works themselves. Because of these two marks a fine work of art is often confused with something which is not art at all. Seeing and avoiding the confusions will help to bring out what is most important in the making of works of art.

(1) Because works of art affect us, some have held that an artist is a technician. He is intent on producing an effect in us and he is skilled and practical enough to know how to do it. It is true both that artists are skilled and that they intend their works to have a certain effect. But their skill is not practical; it is creative, and the effect at which artists aim is to make a work which especially heightens experience aesthetically.

Artistic making is not unskilled. Inner and outer hand, eye, voice, ear and body have all in the practice of creating to be shaped for the making of works of art. Without sustaining or supporting skill, so-called artistic inspiration is never incisive. It cannot surge through us and magically use us to make, without our knowing it, a work of art. Those who are able to make works of art have the inspirations which lead them into still finer making. Those who are not practiced have enthusiasms, perhaps even visions, but these do not of themselves lead to fineness in an art. In art, as in practice, there are no ends apart from means, and our conception of ends is coordinate with means. It is misguided to suppose that inspiration will conjure through its hold on us the means by which an inspired work will in fact be made.

Still, the making of a work of art is not the perfected practice of producing a previsioned result. For all an artist's practice, for all his sketches, models or rehearsals, a work produced in fact is different from a work as planned; no artist ever quite repeats himself. The main reason for this is that a work cannot, apart from the making of it, be thoroughly thought through. And the reason works cannot be thought all through is that a thought does not provide even the major unity in a work of art. Thought deals with a subordinate strand in a work of art, and no matter the guidance it provides, in the making of a work, the creating itself masters and turns the guiding thought. It is not sound, therefore, to think of artistic making as if it were the following of a plan, or a filling of an idea. Whatever idea enters into the making of a work is dominated by the extensiveness of the sensuosities which occur in the work itself. This extensiveness has some closure of itself; it is not boundless, having to be held in by ideas. Such unity as it has of itself prevails over the ideas in fine works of art, but perhaps not tyrannically. Sensitive to such unities, artists (naturally) seem mad to more reasonable men; perhaps they seem undisciplined to men who are skilled in craft. But artistic making need not be less disciplined or skillful than practical production. It can be both disciplined and skillful but still be artistic and not practical at all, even when artists are masters of their materials. Not all mastery need be practical. But this is another argument.

Since the making of a fine work is not dominated by an idea which an artist imposes upon material, artists are sometimes thought to be connoisseurs of materials; they bring out what is intrinsically in the materials themselves: the statue in the stone, the vital rhythms of the body, the purity or movement of a color, a sound, a theme. Here again an artist is likened to a craftsman, or perhaps to a knower who has insight into obscured natural perfections. He uncovers what is already there, or he isolates it, and his skill is in bringing it whole before us. Those of us who are less penetrating can then see things for what they really are; the husks upon their perfections are removed.

What is sound in this view is the obvious note that the artist is attentive to his materials; he respects them and is said to stay within such limits as the materials provide. It is unsound, however, to claim that the artist does not create works of art but that he discovers or uncovers them, that he isolates them, and that works of art are natural beauties set off from obscuring natural or artificial things. Artistry, of course, submits itself to such limits as things provide for us; so does practice, so does reason, so too does religion. Our doing, our thinking and creating are not unrestrained. But then too, none of these leaves what is about us just as it was before. Things are forced to, thought to, and made to have a place inside our activity.

This is true in art even in those modest pieces in which an item of nature is extracted from its natural surroundings and given a border and background and then offered out as a work of art. Such works are compositions, most often only minor ones. In more serious and important works, the unity of the works is not owed to intact materials, nor is it extracted from them. It is created, new and not natural. The sensuosities of materials are what make for the unity, but the unity has to be made—the sensuous has to be shaped, accented, with portions connected to sustain and to be sustained by a subordinate unity. A work has to be singular for us and significant as well. Artists can fail in making too little of their materials, or in making too much of the material's virtuosity; they can also fail in trying to have their materials sustain more than they can, or not enough. But an artist does not merely add something to materials, nor does he remove the dross from what is already there; artistry is not simple arithmetic.

In the making of a work, sensuous materials are to be the content for the ideas which they will overwhelm. The ideas, apart from the work, are definite but general. They guide the making of the work. But they change or are changed as they enter into its making and also as they occur in the complete work. In fine works, ideas are neither imposed on materials nor extracted from them, though it is right that the guiding ideas are kin to the ideas natively in the materials and that finally, such ideas as occur in a fine work are close both to the guiding and resident ones—close, but not exactly the same. The mistaken belief in both the view that creating is imposition and that it is recovery is that the ideas are, throughout, the same. In fact they are not; there are small differences between them, but these make all the difference. Creating is not an adding of something or a subtracting of something from an idea. Materials modify the idea with which they are approached; the ideas they contain are changed as the materials themselves are modified. The result is a work unified aesthetically in which an idea for materials has been embodied and in which a natural intelligibility has been made available for appreciation.

(2) Works of art are not felicitously expressed claims to knowledge. The ideas in them as items of understanding are trivial and obvious. We understand little because of them, but then the fullness of art is not owed to its having us know of things. Art does not represent what knowledge does, nor does it represent in the same way. Many in art are inclined to say that art does not represent at all. This is a negative and defensive view. It means that art does not represent in the way that non-art is thought to represent; it is defensive in trying to defend the autonomy and self-containedness of art—as if one who thinks that art is representative must then treat it as a means and quickly dispense with it when the meaning is finally known. The denial and defense are too extreme. Art is representative in a special way, and we know what it represents only, indeed, as we stay in appreciation of its works. This distinctive representation will be discussed in the next section. For the moment, it is perhaps enough to see that if art represents distinctively and if it represents in prominence something of the real which no other enterprises emphasize, it will of course be distinguished from them and be distinctive in itself. The very making of a work with such a sort of meaning will be the creative act of making a work of art.

The nature of aesthetic experience, then, the bearing of time upon all else, the fecundity of the sensuous, and the distinctive making and meaning of art, all show that art is a basic way of dealing with everything there is. It is on a par with practice, knowledge and religion. Those who love and live in it demean it by protectively suggesting that it deals with what is less than real. Art always deals with what is real, and nothing of reality stands beyond its reach.

SYMBOLS, EXPRESSION AND SIGNIFICANCE

What should we know about significance in art? What questions is it important to ask? We have almost to know their "answers" before we ask them. The reason for this is that questions rest on suppositions, they depend on knowledge of what we are to ask about, and if what we take as known is not true or accurate, the questions built from such a start will be inappropriate. Unfortunately, many questions about significance in the arts do start from unsound views. Perhaps the most interesting of the inappropriate questions is: "How, in general, do works of art tell us of what they are about?" When this question has, without criticism, been accepted and answered, the misguided answer which has most often been given to it is that art tells us what it does indirectly, that works of art are metaphorical, that they are symbols of what is real.

Those who ask this question, those who want to know what art is about and how it tells us what it does, suppose at the start that art is a way of knowing things and that it tells us what they are. For them, the question is simply how all this is done. They raise the question because, supposing that art does tell of things, it seems to tell about them in a way which is different from the telling in our more familiar and less decorated talk. How is it, then, that art does its telling but does it differently from our direct and open claims? The obvious answer is that art is indirect—our familiar claims are direct or literal; the claims in art are metaphorical, and metaphor, as we are all supposed to know, is not the literal beautifully or elaborately expressed. It is the literal expressed in indirection, and because of the indirection, it is richer in meaning than direct speech could ever be. The supposition of the question leads at once to an answer of this sort.

The failures in this view are either (1) that there is no understanding it or (2) that an understanding of it yields a view which

109

is more troublesome than worthwhile. (1) Take a metaphor to have literal but indirectly literal significance and the prized indirection results in a metaphor's not representing anything at all. The indirection makes it impossible to say what, metaphorically, we are speaking of or what is being said. (2) Should it happen though that ingenuities could show that this alleged impossibility is not finally real, the sense of metaphor would have been saved—but it would have been saved by a costly and unattractive change in our view of art. Both these objections should be described in more detail.

(1) Metaphors or symbols, representing literally but indirectly, are supposed to be plainest in the arts which are formed from speech, perhaps in poetry especially. They are said, however, to be the core of every art. We have only to note the terms and the grammars of the arts and then the indirectness of their speech is thought to be quite plain. The indirectness takes one or the other of both of these two forms: (a) we speak of one thing by speaking of something else instead, or (b) we say of something what can properly be said only of a different kind of thing. These forms of indirection are what seem to make symbols so richly meaningful. We are not confined to having them be about or say just this or that; we can take them to be saying any one of several things or many things at once. Since the poet, say, speaks of one thing by speaking of something else, he leaves us free to think just what it is he is finally speaking of. Since what he says can literally be true only of something else, we are also free to think what he might have said about the things he named explicitly. In these ways, metaphors are said to be rich in meaning, and they are thought to guide us in the discovery of what they mean. At last, they mean what they do literally. But their indirectness gives them a range for interpretation which we never find in plainer, literal speech.

Unfortunately, we cannot follow the indirectness to find out what is being spoken of or what is being said. How do we speak of one thing *by* speaking of another? If we are speaking of one thing, we are speaking of it, not of something else, and it is an oddity if not a paradox to claim that we are not really speaking of the thing we are speaking of but of another thing instead. Even then, we've still to understand how, through the indirection, we come to the final subject of our talk. On one side, then, the doctrine of the metaphor is bounded by contradiction, and on the other it leads to an indefinite regression. For if we are not really speaking of what we name, then why should a so-called real subject, whatever it is, be the ultimate subject of our speech: this stands for that which stands in turn for something else, and so on, as if without an end.

The same difficulty, or much the same, holds for what a metaphor is supposed to say. If what we are saying can literally be said only of something else, then, if a metaphor is literal at root, we have to find that something else, and we have also to think what there is to say about the things we have talked about explicitly. Those who press us to appreciate the metaphor acknowledge that what its surface says is false and literally not sensible. They ask us to be patient in interpretation; we are to go beneath the falsity and paradox; we are to find the subtle, buried sense. That sense, they think, is finally literal. But they cannot explain how we get to it, and, in any case, whether literal sense is the distinctive sense in art is not itself so plain.

(2) There are ingenuities, however, by which the sense of metaphor can seem to be preserved. There are many of them, but all of them, in one place or another, make this sort of move: we get over or get through the indirectness in a metaphor by seeing that what a metaphor says explicitly (or what it is explicitly about) is itself something significant. A metaphor is explicitly about signs, and it finally says, or is finally about, whatever the signs are themselves about. This claim would seem to remove the difficulty about indirection, for we can speak of one thing *by* speaking of another if what we first speak about is itself a sign: we are talking of a sign; through it, we are talking of what the sign is itself about. An almost comparable doctrine applies to what is said, and still further ingenuities can be compiled. For example, one term in a metaphor can be thought to represent its object in the same way in which another term of the metaphor represents literally, so that part of a metaphor tells us how, not what, the rest of it represents, and we have again to find its secret meaning for ourselves. According to these ingenuities, then, a work of art is an intricate tableau of signs of signs, and of signs of how we are to understand the signs; there are layers of meaning; we mean

one thing and thereby mean another, with the layers and transitivity in meanings all adding to the richness of the arts.

We can come to understand a good deal about the arts by thinking of their meanings in these ways. Perhaps these are the only ways in which some of us can get at the meanings in works of art. But doctrines about indirectness in representation, however ingenious, always seem to miss something of the arts and to be, even as doctrines, finally unacceptable. They are generous in intent. They want us to see that art is valuable and that its value is that it tells us the truth. They therefore press for the view that the significance in art is literal, even when at first it does not seem to be. At last, though, they go too far.

For one, they finally view the arts as troublesome and dispensable. Why, after all, should we be patient with cumbersome representations? If art is to tell a truth, then let the truth be told straight out. Indirectness and decorative delicacies are distracting and playlike. The plainer, the simpler the declaration of a truth, the better for all of us, and if the indirectness of artists is owed to their not really knowing what they want to say, perhaps it would be best not to indulge them in a fumbling feel for it but to ask that they wait until they are surer and can make their claims most sensibly. Even so, if works of art mean what they do only literally, we are finally to be done with them. When we come to know what they mean, we can turn away from them. Once we have understood them, once we have learned what they have to say and have considered whether they are true or not, we have no further need or use for the works themselves. A view of the significance of art which, as a consequence, sees art as codelike for understanding and as readily dispensable misses much of the significance of art and of the importance of our vital interplay with it.

Then too, as a doctrine, the view that works of art are complicatedly literal either does not get us over the so-called indirectness of art's meaning or if it does, it leaves us with another and an awkward question. The reason the doctrine fails to overcome the indirection is that meanings are not transitive in the way doctrine requires. If A is about B and B is about C, A is not thereby about C. It is about B; its meaning stops right there, with B. B, in turn, can of course be about something, and even though A and B and whatever B is about are then to be connected in meaning, the connections are not linear or transitive. We are therefore not helped to understand the so-called indirectness of reference in a metaphor. If we talk about a sign we are not then talking of whatever that sign is itself about. We are talking of the sign and perhaps saying of it something about the way in which it represents. There is nothing indirect in this. The view that art says literally something about signs but nothing of what the signs are themselves about is interesting. But it is a different view, far removed from doctrines of the metaphor.

Were we to stay with the metaphor, were we to claim to speak of one thing by speaking of another, and to think that the transitivity of meaning is somehow assured, still another awkwardness would show itself. It is that we cannot claim that anything is represented with finality. Suppose A is about C through being about B, what is C about? A will be about that too, and so on, perhaps endlessly. Start the line that A is about what B is about and B is about what C is about, and only arbitrarily is there an end. Let what we are speaking of be itself significant, and let significance be transitive, and there may be nothing that is finally signified. Everything is significant; each item signifies something which signifies something else, and there is a wallow of signifying, and there is no assessment, no consummation in the endlessness of the meaningful. On such a view, we cannot claim for art that, in any way, it represents the real.

No matter how we turn the idea of the metaphor, the idea that it is the vehicle of art's significance at last denigrates the arts. It sees the arts as overcomplicated, dispensable and perhaps not even revelatory of the real. We are driven to talk of symbol or metaphor if we think that there is only one way of representing or saying things, so that everything significant must have its sense in this single style, in some complication or distortion of literal style. At best, the arts could then only have those virtues which are appropriate to literal sense, but these, while considerable, are not enough to give the arts autonomy and irreplaceable value. The arts are not served well, they are not understood, by our play with the ideas of "image," "symbol," or "metaphor." We would do far better to think that works of art have a kind of significance all their own, that they do not represent in an indirect and literal way, but that theirs is a quite different form of representing things. It is a way of representing that is as direct as any way can be—only, what is represented and how it is shown are not the same as what is represented literally. In aim, in execution, in appropriation and consummation, the arts differ from practice, knowledge and religion. Their significance, understandably, should be different too. Is there, then, an account of significance appropriate specifically to art? What is it? How does it proceed?

There have been a number of theories which claim a distinctive mode of significance for art. One of the most important of these is that, in art, feelings and emotions are expressed; little, if anything, is represented, and such representation as is there is incidental or supportive in the arts. Expression is what is central. The appropriate question, therefore, is not "what does art talk about" but "what does it express, and how?" The answer, on this view, is that the artist is moved to make works of art because of his feelings and then, out of the urgency of those feelings or to preserve something of them once the urgencies have passed, he creates works in which the feelings are incorporated. Those who are sensitively responsive to the works are made to undergo the feelings in them. The work controls the generation of the feelings, and their development and accommodation. Appreciating art is an experience dominated by feeling or feeling tone, and we come away from art more or less stabilized in feeling than we were before, more sensitive to some of the things about us, and some of our attitudes are perhaps changed.

In the recent literature, this view has been set out most amply by I. A. Richards. The sciences, Richards says, tell us what things really are. Since the arts are not impressionistic sciences, their intent must be different. Mainly, their import is not to tell us of reality but to shape and steady attitudes; they are to educate and mold our feelings, and forms of artistry should be understood in connection with this aim. Richards acknowledges that some items, here and there in the arts, are indeed literally significant. These, however, serve as posts and turning points for the most important and pervasive sort of speech, for the speech which is emotively charged and which carries tone and engenders feelings in those of us who respond to it. The arts, then, aim to produce aimed feelings and perhaps even more lasting sensitivities. These affect our action. That is why art is important socially. It is aimed at feeling, and feeling starts or stays activity. It is as if, for Richards, we can either know or act, that the sciences alone have to do with knowing and that the arts, as distinct from them, have therefore only to do with our activity; specifically, they have to do with the feelings which precede, accompany and follow our activity. These, the arts engender in us, and this function seems as important as any effected by our thought.

On many points, this is a penetrating view, but it is also a wooden one. The options "thought" and "action" are too narrow to answer to our versatility. Then too, too little of the nature of feelings is made plain. On this view, the word "feeling" labels all, or almost all, of such consciousness as is not the same as thought. But we are not told what differences there are between thought and feeling, and the connections between feeling and action are too obscure. It is as if a feeling were only a lively occurrence inside our heads, that in consciousness it has some special quality, but that it is not caused to occur in the reliably regular way in which thought comes about and it is, therefore, not naturally or properly a sign of what is outside of us. Instead of being useless, mere isolated occurrences without a natural function, feelings are then thought to be connected with activity; their liveliness may prompt or deter activity. The view, then, is mainly a defensive construction. It tells us too little of feeling; it tells us nothing of the meaning in what is emotively meaningful; and it leaves unanswered the questions about which feelings ought to be promoted by the arts and how it is that works of art are excellent and why. If art is not measured against the real which it represents, something else has to ground or test both its importance and our preferences. Nothing, on this view, occupies this crucial place. We are told that in art feelings are important. But why? For what? And in what way? Within the narrow options of this view, none of these questions can be answered well.

A far sounder view has been set out by Suzanne Langer. Mrs. Langer thinks that the arts are representative, but she says that they represent neither the same things, nor in the same way, as do the sciences. The arts are *presentationally significant*. Works of art are ideas of feelings, simulacre of the vitality of life, and they represent these feelings by presenting them to us. They do not speak of them or tell about them. They present them. Then, in our responsiveness to works of art, we both undergo something of the feelings they present and also understand what the feelings are. Art conveys both feeling and understanding, not one or the other exclusively. The distinctive representativeness in art is what enables it to do both—or that is what it is supposed to do. It is on this point that there are a few but important difficulties in Langer's view.

Presentational symbols, according to Langer, present to us something of the feelings they represent. Were they, as it were, to present the feelings themselves, they would not represent them. The feelings would be too close for the telling. Besides, there could be no need to represent them if they are already there. What is it, then, which is presented in or as a work of art? It must be something like a feeling, the quality, the stuff, the form or flow of feeling, perhaps; something less than feeling itself. The question, however, is whether a work of art can be an idea of the fuller feeling of which it contains a part. Can Langer's view answer this question? I do not think it can, and the reason it cannot is that the presented, as a presentation, is not a representative.

Everything sensuous, everything we acknowledge as sensuous, presents itself to us. Works of art do so as well. But rightly to appreciate presented works of art, according to Langer, we have to stay wholly with the presentation and not take the work to have, say, "practical significance." In an "elementary sense," she says, "all art is abstract. Its very substance, quality without practical significance, is an abstraction from material existence." A work of art, then, is an *image*. This is what an artist creates and the whole being of works of art is their visual or auditory or tactile character. "They are, from the standpoint of practical reality, *mere* forms; they exist only for the sense or the imagination that perceives them."

So insulated, though, what can works of art re-present? Nothing, really, or nothing real. They present themselves to us, and their content, as Langer says, is itself their *import*—so the works stand for nothing else. They are too self-contained for that. Were they genuinely to represent, there would have to be some community in being between the works and what they represent. But then, they would not be self-contained; they would not ". . . exist only for the sense or imagination that perceives them."

Mrs. Langer sees works of art as so self-contained that she does not even allow that they might be representative for us because of a concern of ours. That, she seems to think, would be *using* the works, not taking them for themselves. Again, according to her, we are to stay with the enclosed presentations and take them to represent. And what can they represent? Again, nothing real; something virtual, Mrs. Langer says. "The space in which we live and act is not what is treated in art at all . . . it is an entirely visual affair . . . this purely visual space is an illusion." So, too, there is a virtual time and there are virtual powers. These are what are presented and they are presumably representations by being illusory.

The difficulties, here, though, are (1) that since works of art are illusions of nothing real, they are not really illusory, and (2) that he who takes them to be illusory and significant has not really dealt with them as presentations: he was also thinking of something else and thinking that what he is presented with is like what he already knows. He could not otherwise take the presentations as illusory. The presentations, by themselves, in themselves, supposing that there could be such things, are not significant at all. Leaving our concerns aside, the presented as presented is not a representative.

Mrs. Langer's discerning way of insisting on the distinctiveness of art leads her to a consequence of which she herself disapproves —that art is not representative. Partly, she is led to this because she thinks that only science represents the real and that only practice deals with it. Art, for her, must therefore not try to tell us what is really there, nor can it be an instrument in doing things. A work of art has to be something in itself, something less than either a burly physical object or a carrier of messages. The only thing she thinks that it could be is a presentation, self-contained. Such refuge items, though, important as presentations are for art, are too enclosed to be either meaningful or real.

Art, as Mrs. Langer sees, is not science, nor are its works practicalities. But if we see, as she does not, that there is a feature of reality which science and practice do not place in prominence, we can claim that art deals with it, and with all reality through it, and is distinctive in its doing so. We need not make a retreat for art in which its integrity is preciously preserved. We can see, along with Mrs. Langer, the importance of presentation. But we can also hold that art really represents the real. Its simulacre are in likeness to reality; they are not illusions or presentations of virtual objects. The works genuinely represent something apart from themselves. Some of what has already been said about significance, and about the reality of time and our concern for it will provide both the frame and the detail for this final view.

A representation is a part of something else, or it is derived from it or subsumed under it. It is not something wholly in itself. It may signify the larger thing which encloses it. More often, this larger reality will be a context which allows one thing to represent some other thing which might also be a part of the same encompassing entity. These claims were explained and defended in the earlier account of knowledge. They also apply to art—though here, as in the account of knowledge, they have to be specially detailed. The account of time provided in the preceding section, especially the notes about its providing a unity for all things, will help to provide the details we need. The general account of representation together with these notes about time warrant the view that by being a revealing closure of sensuosities, a work of art represents the nature of time and of the other realities which are unified in it.

A work of art is an artificial individual. It is made so as to promote our having an aesthetic experience of it. This is the sort of experience in which the time common to us and to the individual we experience is prominent; the sharp accent of our separate, individual effective agencies is muted and subdued. Works of art are often at first arresting, they stand out as against us. Their strikingness is a challenge to appreciation. In suitable appreciation, the resistant otherness of an individual work is minimized and we submit ourselves to its sensuousness. Doing this is dealing with a work as art.

A fine work of art leads us into itself. When we are in it, we feel its sensuousness and we are also submissive to whatever else is unified in it. The sensuous never occurs alone, no matter how emphatic it is. It is a strand in an experience; in aesthetic experience, it is the major strand. Its extensiveness provides the distinctive unity in such experience; it also unifies such other strands as the experience must also have. An aesthetic experience, then, is as filled with things as an experience of any other kind. It is not, however, as aesthetes are inclined to say, more rich than other sorts of experience.

Sensuosities, sheerly qualitative, are derivative from individuals and they are a merger of the being of the individuals and of the common present time in which the individuals are found. The time common in the individuals is the extensiveness of the sensuosities. As individuals we are not thoroughly distinct from one another even now, though in fact, as fact, we also stand apart. We are merged as beings *in* a common present; we are distinct from one another as we are *at* a present time. It is the merged being, the sensuous, which is the unity in an experience of a work of art. There is some opposition and diversity inside of the experience; the Good penetrates it too. But the prominence of the sensuous is what defines an aesthetic experience as to its kind. Because sensuosities are part of our own being, and because our concern with them is two-sided, sensuosities are also significant. As we will see, they represent the reality with which we are concerned in art, and they do this by incorporating it.

For all the preciousness of singular experiences, those who live in art, like other sorts of men, are concerned not for this or that but for everything. No one is aimed in his whole concern at a limited entity; there would be nothing then that he was concerned to do. Concern, however, has always to be focused. It is thereby, as we have seen before, two-sided: (1) we aim at what we are concerned with through a focused item, and (2) we take the item as a focus because of our concern. The comprehensive reach of our concern is therefore never lost, no matter how preoccupying a focus for it is. No practical man is concerned wholly to do a single thing right now; no thinker is finally content to know or understand one item in isolation from all the rest. The same is true for the artist, in creating his work and in appropriating it appreciatively. The point here is not that an artist is unsatisfied with the latest of his works or that, for everyone, a work of art will finally pall (though these observations are also true). The point is that even in the fulfillment of a creative act or the richness of an appreciative experience, an artist and a viewer are not wholly concerned with what they are then so intensely focused on. Their concern goes beyond the work at hand. The work is in fact significant only because it is a focus for their more comprehensive concern, and it is because their concern is focused in the work that the work itself is, in proper terms, appraised.

For one who lives in art, a work of art is the whole of things reduced; it is a world in small. It is as if the artist were a creator who made a world in which one could live for a time. We address ourselves to art as whole men, not through only a part of us. In turn, a fine work answers to the whole of us. One undergoes it through its sensuosities, and through their depths. Sensuosities have depth because they encompass realities other than individuals and time. These other realities are subordinated to the sensuosities and are unified by them. The sound of the words in a poem, for example, fills out their meanings; the conventional meanings of the words, as if from the underside, strain and texture the supervening sound. To appreciate a work, then, we are to experience it as whole, surface and depth together. As we start toward appreciation, though, we may move from any of a work's constituents—from the strikingness of the work, its appearances, from the ideas in it, or from even the stirring it makes in us. We can move from the partiality of any start to appropriate the fullness of a work. For those who live in art, it is perhaps only when a work is taken in its fullness that it is properly a focus for their concern. The work then shows forth their concern. It thereby represents what they are concerned with, and in being its representative, the work is in small a consummation of the concern itself.

The representation is acknowledged in a resonance, as we feel a work of art to consolidate, and in some fullness to consummate, the concern to have the whole of things be ordered and subordinated in the unity which time provides. Concerned beyond the work, the work itself, as a focus of the concern, is like a chord which enables us to discern our own concern more amply. There is almost a join between a focus for a basic concern and the basic concern itself. This near join, and the resonance of it in a work of art, represents the very realities with which those in art are concerned basically to deal. The work also represents the way in which artists are concerned to deal with them. It does not do so by pointing to the realities and by telling about them or describing them, nor is it directive on how things are to be mastered now and then. In its own way art represents a distinctive unity of realities. A work represents because it is a complex but singular entity whose encompassing unity is provided by its sensuosities. It represents what it does to us because of the concern we have. What it represents are the very realities we are concerned for, unified and enhanced in their unity in the very way we are concerned to have them be enhanced. It does this by quickening to prominence in us the concern we have and by making it more definite. When finally a work palls, that is because it no longer vivifies our concern or because we feel that our concern is not fully or well enough displayed in it.

A work of art, then, is a picture, an icon, an image of something we already feel, though what we feel before we appreciate the work is not felt in special prominence or sensed in good detail. To acknowledge any item as significant we have first to know, apart from it, the very thing it signifies. A significant item is not thereby redundant, or it does not have to be, meaning merely something we already know. It can tell us or show us more about what we already know. True of all significance, this is true of art as well. Apart from an appreciation of any work, those who live in art are concerned in a distinctive way for the whole of things, and it is that array and arrangement of realities which artists take a work of art to represent. It is as if it reminded them of the whole of things and that it quickened and deepened and secured their feel for it. It is their own concern simulated, stimulated, made definite, and as if consummated for a time. A work of art thereby represents the real. In general, it represents time for us and the embrace that time has for all realities. It does this by incorporating these realities inside itself.

This does not mean that a painting cannot present a scene or that a play cannot present recognizable personages and actions. It means that when a painting or a play does this its aim is not to have us understand the scene, but to have us sense the vital spread and configuration in what we then experience, and to take this unity as token of the unity of everything. Turned through the sensuous here and now, a work does not signally signify the special items it seems to be about. It signifies the routes and the embrace with which time enters into them and everything. Is the painting about a house or a bowl of fruit? Is the dance about spring and joy? Of course it is—but what it shows is not these as they are to be understood, intelligible instances of a supervening principle, but these as swelled by the vitalities which sensuosities carry and bind. A work, then, is not an illusion, for what it represents is real. The realities it presents, the unity it pictures them to have, are as real as those we know about or as those we deal with practically. Only, in what it represents and in its way of representing, art differs importantly from the concerns to know and do.

Finally, the claim that a work of art represents time's unifying hold on things allows us to see the soundness in the other, though foreshortened, views of art's meaning which have already been discussed, as if the others were contained inside the claim. For example, there is indeed in art something near to knowledge of the world. Through the ideas which are subordinate unities in it, art reveals something of the structure and intelligible unity of things. Those who are concerned to know will mainly see the ideas in art; perhaps the ideas are all that they will see. This is a great deal to see, still it is not the same as seeing art as art, seeing it distinctively. The arts do not represent in the way in which knowledge does. Something akin to that way is found subordinate in art, and it is what makes for such soundness as there is in the claim that in art we know of things. We go too far, however, if we suppose that art is essentially a way of knowing things and that, unfortunately, the knowing always occurs in distorted forms.

We can also see what is sound in the notion that feeling or emotions are expressed in art. The notion of "expression," as we have seen, is used mainly to suggest an alternative to the claims that art tells us about something other than itself. In denying these, art is then said to do something else instead, to express the feelings which an artist is undergoing or which he underwent and now preserves. Art does not represent the feelings; it does not point to or tell of them; it is not clinical or biographical. It expresses them, and this seems to mean (1) that something like their quality or texture or their form or forcefulness is set out in a work of art, and (2) that they are set out in such a way that it will have done the artist good to have expressed them, and we will also profit from appreciating them. The idea that a work of art reproduces the concern in a life of art can help to make this notion clear and even, indeed, to connect it with the notion of "representation," as the usual view does not. We can hold both that art expresses feeling and that it represents what we have our feelings for. The two stand together in the view that art expresses feeling by representing in a distinctive way.

The themes of "expression" and "representation" connect because a work represents by heightening our sense of our own concern; it thereby heightens our sense of the realities with which we are concerned to deal. Our concern, though always general, has also always to be focused and deepened, made more supple and versatile. We are led by our concern to refine our concern itself; we try to preserve it, but also to modify it with the fullness of whatever enters into the kind of life the concern itself defines. Those feelings which it is supposedly good for art to express—it does not deal with all feelings—are the unresolved and unstable junctures of experience and concern; the feelings are a mark in experience of a lack of adjustment between something in the experience and the concern which defines the experience as to its kind. For artistry, such feeling is analogous to the wonder from which knowing starts, and to the blockage which calls for fresh practicality.

A life in art has its own jeopardies. These are marked by feelings which call for novel activity, which demand of our concern that it be more supply encompassing. The making of a work of art is an activity in response to such feelings. These feelings, these rich disturbances, are made in the creating to have a better place inside an artist's concern. Through incorporating them the concern itself is modified, made more penetrating and definite. This is what explains the saying that when feelings are expressed they are expelled. In fact, however, they are not expelled; it is only their jeopardy to art's concern which is resolved, and this is why it is sometimes said that the expression of our feelings enhances them. In either case, in both cases, as feeling and concern are made more commensurate—they could not be irreconcilably opposed—we sense our own concern more vividly; we feel more fully what it is. To express feelings in a work of art, then, is also to promote that resonance in which our concern itself is made more plain and definite in us. Expression and the sort of representation which is distinctive in art are perhaps not exactly the same. But they are compatible and inseparable. It is, therefore, a mistake to defend art's integrity by saying that a work expresses something but that it in no sense represents. It does both; it can do neither one alone.

Art, then, contains ideas and is effective in us, but it is not the same as knowledge or efficient practice. It means what it does, it does what it does in a way of its own. Not all of us, however, can respond to its characteristic significance. The concern of each of us underlies the sort of significance we find anything to have. Therefore, only those who live in art can deal with things as being distinctively works of art. Others of us respond to it out of our own concerns. We see the arts as more or less effective, as making things more or less intelligible, or as promoting, suitably or not, an enlargement of our spirit. We are tempted then to think of the arts as expressive, intelligible or revealing, but to understand these to be the sorts of significance we encounter in our own practice, knowledge or religion. These understandings are not entirely unsuitable, but they are deeply strained; they verge on being useless in fact and inconsistent in theory, and they even tend to lead us to idolatries. Only those who live in art penetrate the arts as art, and only they feel art to signify in a distinctive way. When we understand what that way is, we can see why and how art has been thought to contain delicately distorted but intelligible metaphors or to be practically effective or effectively expressive. But then we can also see that these views are askew—and see why they are and what is oblique in them. Were we, therefore, finally to raise the issue that was raised at the discussion's start—what do we want to know about art's significance?—our question would have to be: "How is it that works of art picture what is real?" Its answer, I hope it is now clear, is that a work of art is an individual, and that it incorporates and unifies realities in the way in which those who live in art are concerned to deal with the whole of things.

THE FULL LIFE IN ART

The fullness of a life in art is not found in occasional appreciations or even in the making, now and then, of works of art themselves. Those whose lives are in art are not in art only episodically. Art provides range enough for the whole of a life and those who live in art can have their lives fulfilled.

This idea is even now not widely understood. Of all the kinds of lives, the life in art is the last whose shaping we have come to see. That art is important and important to our lives, we have always known. But it has been only in recent times that art has been seen to be comprehensive enough to sustain and fill a life; or perhaps it is that only recently the integrity of a life in art has come to be more plain. In either case, a reason for our not having come widely to see that art can provide for a whole life is that, in earlier times, the perfected arts were subordinated to the concerns of practice and then of religion. Such range as the practice of the arts might have was restricted within urgent practicalities; such devotions as there were in art were restrained in having to conform in other pieties. Where the coerciveness of the state and church were relaxed, art tended more to show that configuration of its own which provides for a whole life. Now, with states being large and with religions being self-preoccupied, its shape is still more evident. We see better what a life in art can be.

To have a life and a kind of life is not merely to be alive. One has to take possession of the life which is in him and refine its natural directedness. The life of anything has some native aim. In fact, most of those who doubt that men naturally have kinds of lives base their suspicion on this belief. Their argument is that all life is of but a single kind, though it is perfected perhaps only in men. Even more strongly, their argument might be that men do not naturally have kinds of lives, any more than animals or plants do. Men are natural beings, and if there are no kinds of lives for animals or plants, the so-called kinds of lives for men are artificial divisions which do not tell us what men are natively. If there are no practical, rational, artistic or religious animals or plants, then none of these kinds can rightly be taken as natural in men. This is a hard argument to answer, but I think it can be fully and soundly opposed. At the start, the opposing answer touches on the oldest of mythic themes; finally, it leads us to say what it is in men which assures us that men naturally have lives of different kinds.

Animals and plants are alive and their lives have native directedness. This directedness has been called an aim, and it is something like an aim. Still, it does not provide for kinds of lives among the members of a species, and an aim is not the same as a concern. There is, however, a fair or strong kinship between the lives of animals and plants and the kinds of lives which we humans have. The kinship is so close that myth, legend, dim consciousness, fantasy and fancy often suppose that all the living have the kinds of lives we do. The bee, the ant, the beaver are busy doing things, and bulls are brute in their virility; it would be incongruous if even one of them delighted in pretty sights or softened charms. Owls are wise, peacocks plume themselves, and the serpent is a mystery. This old and ready reading shows that the kinds of lives we have, or something kin to them, are found among the animals. The kinds are perhaps not developed in them with pronounced distinctiveness. But that something of them is there cannot be a whole fiction; we could not otherwise, with such striking uniformity, read our kinship into them. Even if strictest accuracy were, therefore, to lead us to say that, really, there are no kinds of lives among the animals and plants, there would still be no bar to our thinking that men have kinds of lives, or even that, among living things, men alone have them. For even if animal and plant natures do not divide into kinds of lives, they show at least the definite hues of the different lives, and that is enough to have us see that men are not exceptional beyond all reach.

But men are after all strikingly different from other living things. Alone among them, or pre-eminently among them, we have kinds of lives. The reason for this is that we have not merely an aim but a concern. We are not merely pointed at something or under its governance or restraint. There is also something we are concerned to do, and we are thereby representatives of one or another of the basic realities. Animals are sensitive to the significance of things. We, however, take ourselves to be significant— as representatives of history, as having principles or as standing for the truth, as disciples of Apollo, or as being specially created in the image of God. It is the fact that we are representatives of the basic realities which defines us distinctively, and it is in being representatives that our lives are divided into different kinds.

What is it to be a representative being? It is not simply to be conscious or self-conscious, though consciousness is no doubt part of our being representative. Notions of consciousness and self-consciousness have dominated modern thought about the nature of man. No discussions of them, though, have been more penetrating than those with which Descartes began our thought about these themes. To be conscious, on his view, is to have items be significant; and to be self-conscious is to acknowledge one's self as significant, as a mind, or, finally, as an image of God. The reference to God, in Descartes, is to explain how it is that things are genuinely significant, and how it is that we can be by being significant. The notion that we are minds and spectators of ideas is but a special case of Descartes' far wider claim—that we are shaped by some basic reality or have it incorporated in us, that because of this basic reality we find that other sorts of things are significant for us, and that we ourselves are significant: we are representative in representing the reality which grounds the significance that things have for us.

This cartesian conclusion, or the form of it, helps us to understand how it is that we are representatives. We are representative by representing—by representing the reality which makes it possible for other things to be significant for us. How we ourselves represent this reality depends on the sort of significance the reality is the condition for. We need not be an image of it. Descartes' themes provide for us wider scope than that.

However, we are not representatives of a basic reality only through our representing it. We also represent it by acting on its behalf. We are active beings, concerned to deal with everything through the basic reality we represent, and we are concerned to have it ordered and suffused by that reality. It is therefore, as if we were that very reality transfixed, or an instrument of it, an instance or embodiment of it, a creation, or an incarnation of it. We show it forth just by being, by acting in a certain way. To have a life, then, is to possess and direct the life which is in us; a basic reality provides its native directedness, and we have a kind of life because we are concerned, not merely aimed, and because we represent a basic reality, and we act as it does, or in its behalf, to unify the whole of things.

These reflections, even though tormentedly abstract, should help us to see not only what is meant by a kind of life but how a kind of life can be full or excellent. We already see this well enough, perhaps, for practice, knowledge and religion; many have made the richness of these lives clear. We seem to see it less for the life in art. To many of us, art seems to provide only a thinnish life, effete and removed; it seems too sporadic and unstable to define a life for a whole man. What we should see to correct such views is that art can reach as far and deep as any kind of life; it can be as fulfilling as the concerns which animate men of other kinds. It too is a dealing with the whole of things.

One side of this comprehensiveness is seen in the fact that, for men who live in art, everything is appreciated aesthetically. What a practical man would praise for its efficiency, an artist might see as having grace and rhythmical harmony; his analogue for rational cogency will be lucidity, or perhaps the felt swell of things in an aesthetic unity; and many find themselves attracted to what religious men think of as worship because of the poetry of the ritual and the drama of the sacraments. Nothing lies beyond the reach of appreciation. A man can, as it were, be a pair of eyes, a Zhivago, who sees everything and finds in each, for all its corruption, danger and misuse, some mark of what he feels as beautiful. A man can be a pair of ears for whom, despite the overtones, there is music everywhere. The senses reach as far and penetrate as deep as hands or head or heart, and through them we may feel ourselves close to the vital core of life.

The reason for claiming that the senses have this reach is simply that everything has some bearing on time in a present's sensuosities. Men who are not in art tend to leave the sensuous aside or to make it subordinate in their own and in different kinds of activity. For men of art, however, the sensuous provides the major unity in experience. For them, every act is appreciative. Since everything shows itself through the experiences which are unified by sensuosities, appreciations can reach to everything. And so they should. Or rather, there is no neutral ground or overriding principle which rules that this or that should not be dealt with appreciatively.

Those who appreciate create acts of appreciation, and the making of their own lives is the art of making a life into a work of art. Indeed, this is perhaps the best brief way to understand a life in art: we live in art if our activity is made, appreciatively, to have a supervening sensuous quality and if our lives themselves are made to be works of art. But now, to go further, to think about lives lived with works of art and about the fulfillment which they lend our lives, difficult issues about the "size" of works of art and their meanings must be raised. The fullest life in art, or the most excellent, is lived within works which are large enough to contain us.

One can think of short poems and brief songs, small but precious things, rich with all the meaning they condense. There are also larger works, proportioned monumentally, epics, buildings, operas. Still further, the most ambitious reach of art is to take the dross from men and from all the world, and to have our lives, our thoughts and feelings, our possessions and our communities take their finest grace as art. Nothing less can satisfy men who live in art. The older Pygmalion brought art to life; the modern Pygmalion brought life to its fullest firmness as a work of art. Art is nearer now to doing what art always dreamed to do—to proportion the entire range of things.

There has been very little thought about the scale of works of art, and questions about proper size are easily misunderstood. Poe and a few others have, however, made the issues clear. They have asked how long a poem should be. What may poetry as poetry properly undertake? What length is appropriate for its intent? If a work of art is unified through its sensuosities and these are always of some extensiveness, it is a question for us how much and what can be held within the spread of distinctive sensuosities. A general answer to these questions will, of course, not be a good guide for critical appreciation. In specific cases, we trust both to a natural and a tutored feel for things. Models of buildings, of men and of some animals are, though perhaps attractive, too small in scale to be excellent as works of art. A song may sing of spring but the seasons need a symphony. Portraits have a proper size. Novels can be too short or long. Large cartoons are silly or boring, and a suburban lot is too small for a Mt. Vernon, no matter how reduced its scale. There is a size appropriate to different works and this size bears on the meaning of a work and the fullness it can make within our lives.

Questions about the meaning of works of art arise mainly about small works, about those that we can encompass, look at, listen to or walk around. However appreciative we are of them, however aesthetic our experience of them may be, the works are individuals; they are apart from us and they seem never to mean enough. If they are fine and we are toned and trained to be sensitive enough, there is a resonance in us which is caused by what we appreciatively discern in them. This does not satisfy us fully, though. Our preoccupation with their meaning is to find a way in which the works can *be,* not merely *mean,* more for us, so that the works and what they mean will together satisfy the whole of us. It is as if we want to deal with the whole of things and that when we see ourselves as confronting something limited, we also try to see it as a sign of whatever else there is. Ingeniously, not mistakenly, time and time again, we find the whole of things in small. Important as microcosms are, we are insatiable in wanting more.

With larger works there is less urgency about meaning, and this is an important fact. We are not as inclined to ask about the meaning of a symphony as we are about the meaning of a shorter piece. The same is true for novels and stories, buildings and statues, ballets and dances. In general, regardless of the kind of art, largeness of scale affects us so that we are less concerned to know what the works might mean. The reason for this is that we live more fully with the larger pieces; we are not, as it were, at a distance from them, as we are with smaller, shorter, flatter works. We have to commune with small works as distant singulars or singulars soon past; we have them as isolated and then we want them to mean what their isolation makes them exclude. Larger works envelop us and prevent the intrusion on us of what is not a work of art. While distinct from them, we find ourselves in them, living there, so much so indeed that the works which we create seem in their own way to be creative, to make us part of themselves, to create a world of art in which we ourselves are made to be what we are by art. This is the special case in art of the general principle that what we make, the kind of thing we make, makes us in turn.

Architects and city planners, more than other individual artists, are especially concerned with the meaning and effect of scale. They see that buildings and cities and an environing nature surround us, that we live inside of them and there is little of us which these surroundings do not affect. Their vision leads us to imagine the widest life in art—a whole people, a community, becoming the artist which makes of and for itself a life which is, and in which we are, a work of art.

No one is by nature a New Yorker or a Texan, though one

place rather than another might be more congenial to us. We are touched by places differently, depending on the kinds of men we are. Socrates said that he learned from men, not trees. In different places, different castes of mind occur, and there are different styles and tastes. Prophets come from an austere land; cities, so the prophets charge, rot our spirits and lead us far astray. A human being, civil, rational or spiritual, as an artist sees him, is partly an artifact and the artistry can be good or not.

Now we have architects and city planners. In the future, there will perhaps be still wider artists, and perhaps we will also have artists who explore and shape our common depths: there will be artists for regions, nations and the world; there may be artists who make us feel the vital pulse of our communal lives. These artists of breadth and depth, we as a community of artists, will strain to shape the whole of things. Nothing is outside the intent of such artistry—cosmetics and costume, manners and speech, foods of fineness and delights of sight, streets and buildings whose spaces are inviting, exciting, and which give us now and then repose; apertures for nature, fast and slow, intricate and simple, rhythms and contrasts in public and places for our privacies. Art, reaching this far, shaping practice, thought and faith, is in its own way as ambitious as practice, as rational as mind and as dedicated as religion. Each kind of life, reached full, seems more and more like the other kinds of lives. When art has this extent, questions of the meaning of our art lessen and finally no longer have a place. The reason for this is that when art holds everything inside itself, there is nothing else for it to mean.

It is the concern we have in art which makes things art for us; it also makes us works of art and it provides for the distinctive meaning in the arts. In appreciating works of smallish scale, our concern is quickened and the resonance of the works with our own concern shows what we feel the works to mean. We have a larger life inside works of larger scale. There, our concern is not brought to life merely now and then but is played out all the time. The widest world of art would be the world in which our concern is fully shown; it is the world in which the reality at which we aim in art is made to have the prominence we are concerned that it shall have. In its fullest reach, it is, of course, still partly an ideal.

Occasional appreciations and the recreative arts and hobbies are not the stuff of a full life in art. A kind of life is defined by a concern and our lives are full as we are able with the full range of our powers to represent the reality through which we take our aim. Gallery goers and hobbyists, unless their visits and activities are displays of their concern in minor roles, have fragmented lives; their lives are single only in the loosest sense and they are hardly ever full. A full life is one life, one in concern, of course, as all lives are, but one life in also having one's whole being tested full as over against all the realities which are inside a concern. We cannot be full men or have full lives if we emasculate from our lives the intrusive threat to our concern which the full range of realities provides. We have instead to risk the fragmentation these realities threaten to produce and to make them into instruments and outcomes of our concerns. We aim in our concern at everything and through everything at the reality with which we are concerned, and our lives are full as this is done without reserve. Aristotle supposed that men of virtue act upon the single principle of their nature. Plato thought that the Good provided the proper single order for the soul. Kierkegaard enjoined that we shall will one thing. No less singularity is appropriate for the life of art. In its concern, all that we are can find the distinctive consummation of an art.

Chapter V

The Sacramental World

———

Few of us nowadays understand the religious life. Few of us think that it is beautiful, or that it is vital in the world. These responses are not altogether inappropriate. Religion has recently become dark, thick and slowed. It has not been shaped so that we can live in it fully as contemporary men, and as a partial life it has come to seem removed.

There are many reasons why religion has not taken contour in modern times. One of them is simply that other sorts of lives have recently become more prominent; there are options now we did not have years ago. Nonreligious men in the past had often to shape themselves inside religious communities. Generous as those communities may have been, nonreligious men were always out of tune with them. Now they can make different measures of their lives. Religious men are the ones who do not fit well into the new public forms of life and, from its inner side, religion has

133

not been discerning, supple and loving enough to fill and overflow these forms.

There are many causes for this. Weaker, less able men have come into religious institutions; such service no longer seems the "proper" place for the first of the "well born." Discipline of the spirit has been neglected, as if it were settled that there are suitable courses for developing our bodies and our minds, but that religion will come to us all at once when God seizes us unexpectedly. Then too, religion has not been vitalized by the arts. Even though our places and practice of worship have been made more attractive, the arts have not penetrated our devotion, nor, except by supplying large decorative schemes, has religion much shaped the arts. Finally, there has been less and less theology, and even then most of the recent work is apologetic and niggling. We have been quickened about every other dimension of things by new insights and sensitivity. Yet to many of us it would seem sacrilegious to suppose that there can be new discoveries about God. Religion has failed to win for itself fresh support from practice, thought and art. Religious life has thinned accordingly.

Still, it is possible to see the larger outline of a religious life. Like other sorts of lives, the religious life is ample enough to allow for variety. There is, however, a single configuration which all the varieties adapt. It is to aim at everything through the entry to it which God provides and to aim, as well, at everything so as to come close to God himself. This two-sidedness of the religious life is expressed in the Christian injunction to love God and our neighbor. It is expressed, of course, in other Western religions too.

God is and provides an access to everything. Some theologians explain this access by saying that God created the whole of things, that apart from him things have no being of their own. Even the principles of rationality are said to be without separate standing; they are ideas in the mind of God. Time, too, its passage, is said to be part of God's creativity. These explanations, however, can be only partly right, and it would be a misconception of mystery to insist that they are surely sound, but that an understanding of their meaning and of their soundness is forever beyond our reach. To say that something of God's is mysterious is to talk of the demeanor in which God is most appropriately approached. It is not to say that in not understanding we understand all that can be known. God can be understood to be an access to everything without supposing that the whole being of things derives from him. On that supposition, very little can be understood—the meaning of creation, for example, or of love, sin, service, suffering, redemption, providence or immorality. These things can indeed only be understood by supposing that God is not the only access to the real. There is no threat to genuine religiousness in seeing God as one among other realities. Beside him, there are other routes to things as well, and some of us are naturally inclined to them.

God cannot or could not ever have been the whole of reality—though those who see that everything is suffused by him can, understandably, have come to hold this view. Nor can God have created everything—though we have to look to him to see how it is that things persist and that there is a meaning in history and in the course of time. Nor can it be that God provides the light of our knowledge or prescribes how all of us shall act—though it is true that there are revelations and that, if we are religiously concerned, God's bearing upon the world will show itself in the form of law.

These reservations upon traditional claims should be developed in a full theology. No more than a hint of that theology has been given either here or in the earlier discussion of God's reality. The central claim of the theological part of this philosophy is that God is not the sole or the pre-eminent reality. He is perhaps the most self-contained of singular entities, but even so, there are realities apart from him. He bears upon all the others and they in turn provide him with roles he would not have if they were not finally real. Many a traditional theologian wants to say that God gets angry with us or that he loves us, that he suffers for and because of us, that he sustains us and then draws us to him, that he incarnates himself in the world and that he courses through it, lending it a providential time. None of this could be understood if God were the only or the pre-eminent reality.

It is no slight to religion to amend an exaggerated claim that has been made on its behalf. Men in modern times have made exaggerated claims on behalf of politics; it is only now that we are coming to loosen them. The Greeks and the rationalists seemed to misconstrue the Good through which we come to know of things. Romantics were extravagant about the arts. A number of religious men have been in error too. The corrective claim that God, while real, is not the sole or pre-eminent reality preserves for us much of the insight in the devotions of religious men. It does indeed allow, as many religious men deny, that through realities other than God we may deal with the whole of things. But it nevertheless also sets out what is essential for defining a religious life: that God bears on everything, that he provides an access to everything, and that acting through him and toward him we can have the singularity of a life.

The religious life was apparently discovered by the Jews, or at least, ill fitting as they first found it, it was brought to special clarity by them. They, of course, were not the first to think of God as singular. Their achievement was rather to see that a singular God can be the focus for a whole life. Those who try to serve many gods are fragmented men; they cannot reconcile in religion the different pulls on them, and any other reconciliation leads to a different kind of life, as the torments of Greek religion show. Those in the East, on the other hand, who feel that final being has no confrontations, oppositions or distances within it, aim—and oddly so—at not being men and at not having human lives. Singular men, a singular God, or else no religious life; there is no alternative. The Jews, separately and together, in fervor and failing, drew out for us the configuration of a religious life. They seemed to see that God can reach into everything and that his can be the most insistent of demands. They also saw how, aimed at him and through him, we can bring everything inside our lives.

The Jews seemed to think that God has to allow us to go at things through the access to them which he provides. One has, as it were, to be chosen; God himself has to open his access for our use. This idea is also found in the notion that God shows us who he is, tells us how to pray, establishes his church, and points out to us what is to be done. God's allowance is, or is signaled in, a covenant. In a covenant, we are not made identical with God, but such of his bearing upon things, as can be made part of our own way of dealing with them is opened up to us. The covenant issues in a law; for us, God's bearing upon the whole of things takes the form of law. Which law, what single law, how pointed, detailed or divided, has always concerned religious consciousness. The Jews moved uneasily between enormous complications of the law and the very simple statements made of it by such rabbis as Hillel. They would have us see that law reaches through each nuance of a life and yet also embraces life overall. Christians, with what they feel is a sure hold of the law in general, have only with reluctance set out law specifically. They try to feel God's way toward each specific case, guided by the sureness they find in the incarnation of a Christ. All religious men, regardless of their sect, try to take God's way with things by following his law, by pledging that his will, not our own insofar as it is wayward, shall be done, by being his children, his servants, soldiers in his cause.

Our traditional religions are so emphatic about the clearness of God's way that they are not as responsive as they should be to the man who is caught up in the world and who is seeking, even if he would perhaps not acknowledge it, to see the face of God. A man must indeed stand alone before God. But other men can help him to find God and they can steady him as he comes to take his stand. Most of our religious institutions, though, concern themselves with their own members, or with those who are likely to become members soon. They are not much occupied with people outside their church. When they have gone out to them, their mission has too often been to celebrate the truth as all revealed. They offer quick arguments, full doctrines; bright beauties, promises and threats. Intimations, thoughts, threats and promises may indeed loosen and aim a latent religiousness—but they do not do so as easily as conventionally pious men suppose and, even so, they only start one on his way. He who is religious has not only to act in accord with God but to seek to be with him as well. This task is so awesome that some believe it cannot be achieved by a man alone; he needs the help, the reaching openness of God himself. No one is sure, however, how far one has to travel before this grace will come, and some of the Talmudists, Augustine, St. Theresa and a few others have shown us that devotions have to be endless even if one is sure of God's savingness. No one masters the world in practice; none comes to know it through and through; none captures it entirely in a work of art. So there always has to be distention, distortion, sin of some kind

in a religious life. The distance between a man and God cannot
be entirely overcome, even if and when he is saved.

Religious men are caught between God and other things. They
have ever to come close to God, to see him, and to stand before
him. They must also address others in accord with God's will.
They may stress one of these "directions" more than the other,
but there is inescapable risk, uncertainty and presumption in doing so. One who retreats to perfect his piety and to pray on our
behalf may not make himself pure enough to be our representative; he may move very far from God because of pride. One who
ventures into worldly things on God's behalf risks losing sight
and sound of him. It is not always God's work which is done in
his name, with what hurt to God we are not sure. Crusades have
flattened the world and it is not clear that they have done it any
good. There is no surety for religious men, no matter their emphasis, their boldness, their quiet retreat. The threat for them is
that what they do may not be acceptable in God's sight. No sign
for them can be sure, or sure for very long. The threat may be
heavy and ominous at times; at others, and dangerously, it does
not press them much. It is however always there, a torment
inescapable.

Some religious men can keep themselves in patience in the
world. Their faith is firm, unbelief is stayed. No matter the seeming chaos of things, no matter the brutality and lack of sense,
God, they think, will show himself and a remnant will be saved.
For others of no less firm or fine a faith, there is no sureness for
the world. The peril is that God can forsake the world and that
he always has cause enough to leave. Because of sin and imperfection, we are not thought to deserve the gift which God bestows
on us, and none of us can demand that God shall not withdraw.
Some, of course, believe that he will not depart. In spite of everything, he made a covenant with a people, or sent his son to redeem
the world, or he established his church within it, or his spirit
courses through and sustains the world. Others, like David, or
Paul or Kierkegaard keep their faith even in their unsureness and
unbelief. For them and others the threat that God will withdraw
is always real and, sometimes, it may have seemed to come to
pass. Men may feel that God has hidden from the world, that the
shikina, the spirit, has passed from the land. It may even seem

to some that there is no God at all. In that great terror, some men cannot sustain themselves. They may think that all along their devotion was misplaced, that really, there is no sin, no holy imperfection, no divine eternity, and no ultimate demand that men be saints. Instead, there is only wrong doing, or error, or indelicacy—and these, the only failures, are not a trespass against what is divine but failures in a search for a different triumph over time. It may seem that men are not imperfect but only weak, not evil but only inefficient, dull and gross, and that their obligation was never to be holy but to have perfection of a different kind. To men for whom all this seems true, a life in faith is not open to their humanity. They have to focus better their concern, be as if born again, and affirm themselves as members of a different world.

The most poignant record we have of the torment of a religious man is the story of Job. In the face of loss, accusation, loneliness and hurt, Job retains his faith. The story has often been studied. It is full enough, however, to bear still further thought. It will show us not only the torment there can be in a religious life, but the meaning and the promise of such a life as well.

THE STORY OF JOB

Scholars have divided the story of Job into pieces. They have pointed out that parts of it were written at different times and that these differ in vocabulary, phrasing and emphasis. These discoveries—important as they are—have not made the story easier to penetrate. One suggestion, often made in connection with the discoveries, has in fact made it harder to understand. It is that we should attend only to the original, the core of the story, and dispense with its added and disturbing beginning and end: that God should wager, yield power to Satan and, out of vanity, allow Job to suffer seems not religiously revealing but outrageous and impermissible; that Job should at the end have health and wealth restored seems impertinent and distracting, as if God were trying to make Job forget values that are lost and irreplaceable. Still, crude though the beginning and end may be and crudely drawn, they are essential both to there being a story and to making out the meaning of Job's loss. The center, the core, is not itself a story; nor does it show us all we need to see. We should come to see the story whole.

Even as a whole, however, the Book of Job is hard to understand, because the book fights against itself. It repudiates one scheme of thought but it does not entirely escape from it. It repudiates the theme that God commands, that men are to obey, and that failing that they are punished and made thereby more attentive to God's ordinance. The denial is simply that the man who obeys religious injunctions need not have a brimming and blessed life and that catastrophe, loss and great pain are not a sure sign that a commandment has been broken.

The question remains, though, God being God, how are we to understand pain or suffering if they are not punishment? The book claims that these have to be interpreted but it does not tell us how. It thinks solely of obedience and reward, disobedience and punishment; it knows that these are not the right dimensions of the religious life, but it sees no alternative to them. Is there an alternative? There seems to be, and to bring it out I want to (1) review the events of the book which are to be interpreted, (2) see how and why they are understood the way they are, and then (3) note the one-sidedness of the interpretation and set out the other, the neglected and finally helpful side.

(1) The Book of Job is about the strain and torment that test and deepen a religious life. It is about how a religious man interprets his own actions and what he undergoes. For one who lives in God, every event is a consummation and a portent. Some events, however, are particularly revealing, and the book deals most with these—with the loss of children and great goods, and with the meaning of prolonged pain. It is inattentive to the death of servants, the pain of animals and ravage to the land. Job's losses, his pain, are what are to be understood.

(2) Everyone in the book believes that to make out the meaning of Job's losses, they are to look to God. The comforters say that Job's suffering is punishment. They take this view because they believe that the suffering is caused by God and that the cause explains the nature of the effect. Thinking that God rewards and punishes, they have to hold that Job has transgressed an ordinance and that he has been punished, and punished all the more for his

stiff-necked lack of penance. The losses are what God intended, and their special severity is to make God's meaning much more clear. The comforters are right to see God as efficacious; they are right to see that religious men are to align themselves with him; they are also right to see that there is something wrong in the stance which Job assumes. Much of their advice is sound.

Job, however, sees nothing in what they say. Granted, their tone is strident and they are inflexible; they are reprimanded at the end. But Job sees no further than they see and he loses hold even of their sense. As against them, he says that he has not violated any law and that, presumptuous but not impious, he therefore has a case before the Lord. Such indictment as there is against him has to be explained. Nothing so far shown reveals that he has transgressed against the law. His suffering must have a meaning. But what violation makes it meaningful? What is the suffering if not punishment? Job knows no other meaning for the fact. Yet it is another meaning, another sort of meaning, which helps us to find the sense of the whole book.

(3) What helps us is the idea that a religious man is to look to God for the meaning of what occurs, but he is not to think of God as the cause of any fact. God does indeed help in forming what occurs, or so it seems, but he is not the entire cause of such occurrences. What occurs, therefore, is not a sure sign of God's intent. Job's comforters connect the meaning and the cause of what occurs too closely together. How is the connection to be loosened but still to hold? There has to be some connection between God and what happens in the world; an appeal to God for meaning would otherwise be useless or irrelevant. The connection we should see for Job, however, is not a causal one. It is the other side of the theme of God's causality—it has to do with the fact that through our dealings with worldly things we come to stand near to God, or far from him, and perhaps to affect him in our doing so.

Why both these sides? Because a religious man aims both (a) at everything through God and (b) toward God through everything else. The idea of God's rewards and punishments emphasizes the first side of this task and says of the other only that how one stands to God depends on his having done what God ordains or not. The poignancy in the Job story comes not with this first side, but in its emphasis on the second. If we are aimed to be near God, everything, everything we do, testifies to where we are. Things have meaning not only as a result of God's intent; they also show where we are in the task of moving close to him. God's intent for us can be read in what happens in the world. But our intent for God can be read there too. We have to look to God for meanings of both sorts. We have, however, to look in different ways. We can ask both what something shows about God's intent, or about our own intent to reach toward God himself. In the second of these ways, everything is for us a trial. If we are intent on God, everything we encounter or undergo is made by us into a means for reaching him. Each is a test, trying our devotion, showing how we stand to God. The meanings in Job's losses and his suffering come from their being trials. They show us how Job is a man of God. This is near to what Job himself comes at last to see.

Job's children have been killed. What shall it mean to a man that his children die? Is anything to have a meaning for him with them gone? But then, where does his devotion lie? How firm can it be? Abraham was tested by the threat to his child's life. Jesus enjoined that the dead shall bury the dead and that there has yet to be a life. So too for Job. His children are not the meaning of his life. No man's children are. He does not live for them. Even when he lives through them, his life is his own and, religiously, it is aimed toward God. The children surround the devotion; they are a blessing which sweetens it, and they also try it some. Their death tests the depth and steadiness of the devotion. It shows Job his own trust. Job rents his robe, shaves his head, falls upon the ground. As we know, he is supposed to have said "the Lord gave, and the Lord has taken away; blessed be the name of the Lord."

Pain drives us in upon ourselves. It is one of the severest trials. It makes us so self-absorbed that we may not see anything except ourselves. To escape it, we will turn to anything, turn away from anything. Pain, therefore, tests our directedness. Will we stay aimed in the way we had been? How were we really aimed? Will we through the pain come to even greater steadiness, or will we turn so wholly in ourselves that the pain, not we, comes to have our life. Satan knows what pain can do. He says "skin for skin! All that a man has he will give for his life. But put forth thy hand now and touch his bone and his flesh, and he will curse thee to thy face." When Job is covered with loathsome sores, his wife says that he should not hold fast to his integrity but should curse God and die. Job, in this, "did not sin with his lips." Yet he was not blameless. His heart was not altogether clear. Misguidedly, he wanted his pain to reveal what it never could have showed.

Death and pain and loss are signs to a religious man of where he is and how he stands with God. They signify his route and his place on it. They can help him further to find his way. They do not reveal very much of God. It is as we are directed to God that they are especially significant. But they do not show a man why he is where he is or why they themselves are there. God is a condition of their being significant but his way with things is not much revealed in them. Yet this is what Job most wants to know. His trust is firm, but it is impatient, indignant and distorted. The way Job's demand is finally answered is in his seeing God. He then sees, not that God's way with him was right, but that one's trust in God, one's aim toward him, shall be without hedge, reservation, promise or demand. It is a rending error to think that at the end of the book we are to see that God parcels justice out to us no matter how things appear, only that his justice is more mysterious than we can understand. Say this and we say that Job's comforters were all along quite right and that the story is simply about hard punishment for an unnamed wrong. The point is different; the disclosure shows something else. It should not be read to show that God intimidates Job so that he no longer dares to ask what he wanted all along to know. It shows instead that God can or should be the focus for the whole of a life and that to be a religious man one is to have no sight for anything except in the love of God.

This last point is important in feeling for the texture of the religious life. No man is sure how he is to come to God. It is not enough to do God's ordinance, even if one knows the law. One has as well to come to God in doing it, and it is never sure to us if this is being done. God can seem, however near at hand, at infinite remove. Everything, everything we do, can then be searched through as a sign of where we are, as a token of the depth or purity of our concern and a test of its aim. A man aimed at God lives inside his aim and there is no question for him why or whether he should be there. He has to bear whatever comes within this kind of life. What one takes as tests may show him that he never was a religious man; this was seen before. But for one who is religious, tests always show something else. They show how one stands to God, where he is in a life shaped by a concern which is aimed at him.

We have to accept the conditions which define the kind of life we have. Much within the lives can, of course, be changed but not everything is changeable. What cannot be changed has simply to be borne. The torment comes in seeing how much and what can be changed while concern remains the same. Where are the contingencies in our lives? How are these suffused and where are they bounded by what cannot be changed? Here, we can only feel our way. And no one of us can demand of God that he shall suffuse our lives this far and in a specific way. It is not that we are puny and have no claim on God. For all that is true in this, it is also true that there are limits on God's reach. We stand apart from him and he has to leave us be that way; he cannot dominate us through and through and still have us be in search of him. Men may aim toward God, and he seems to move toward us as well. But there is no sureness about the overlap between the two. God, as some have claimed, suffers because men do not come to him; men suffer because they cannot find that God is everywhere supporting them. The mid-ground between God and man is, so to say, not firmly held by either one, and in that region there are no guarantees. One might even without presumption wager on what will happen there. The wager is an open one; neither God nor man can know in full what will come about. Both, however, have to keep their aim no matter what the result.

No man, then, can ask of God that his life shall be in brimming measure bountiful. It is not inappropriate, however, to search for a sign that the religious life, whatever may come into it, answers fully to our natures, that it provides for a full life. In miscast form, this is what Job was asking for. At the end, seeing God, Job also saw that his own questions had been misaimed. He was not then deterred from asking them. Rather, he saw that all the while he was looking for something else and, finally, he saw what it was that he was looking for: God is God, men are to stand before him, and a religious life is as full as a life for men can be. What is searched for, then, is not the assurance that the religious life is good or that such a life will be filled with health or pleasure or rewards. Such a search would be an impiety; it would see religion as a means to something else. What is wanted instead is a sign from the inside of the religious life that the religious life is full in its demand on men.

The partiality and incompleteness of our lives can be felt and acknowledged for what it is. Many of us feel that our lives can be fuller than they are even though we do not know what will fill us up. It is as if we hungered for something more. If the religious life can complete us, then, it should testify to its fullness, or we can search for a sign of its being fulfilling. The sign can be found, perhaps, in the feeling that there is ever more to do, not in busyness of course, but in what is open to us and calls for being done. It might be found in the feeling that we have failed or have ever to fail, even that we "despise" ourselves and "repent in dust and ashes." There are perhaps other signs as well. It would not even be a great blunder to suppose that the fullness of a religious life can be shown in fortunes and blessings. These come at last to Job. But then he, if not his friends, reads them differently than they were read before.

These suggestions about meanings, causes and testimony may help us to see the Book of Job as a whole. We know nothing of the motives of those who added to the book, but it may be that they aimed, not to exempt God from injustice or other failings, or to soften the effect of Job's loss, but simply to make out more fully what seems to them the story, the truth, about God and Job. If we read the Book of Job as a whole and with the suggestions here, we should see (1) that God does not cause Job's losses. It is not even inappropriate to imagine that God wagers that Job will sustain his devotion no matter what occurs, and it is a sign of Satan's sure sight that Job's severest trials are to lose his children and to suffer in prolonged pain. (2) It is also right to see with Job's wife and his comforters that we are to look to God to make out the meaning of Job's loss. Their view of the meaning is wrong, but they are not wrong in charging that there is something ill-fitting in Job's stand before the Lord. (3) The meaning of Job's suffering is not punishment, though it resembles that. The meaning is the meaning revealed in a test, a trial. It is not properly read by Job at first. Like the comforters, Job is inclined to think that the religious life is lived through obedience to ordinance and that its fullness is shown in manifest blessing. He comes later to read the signs to show how far he is from God but that even so his life is beyond other measure full. (4) The comforters do not understand the demand of the religious life; it is therefore appropriate that they are finally corrected. They were, however, all along right to see that Job is to live differently than he did before, and Job himself comes to see this; his stance and petition are to be fuller and more patient than they were. (5) He who is religious, Job sees, cannot ask that this or that be done for him. (6) There can, however, be the assurance that the religious life, no matter what occurs inside of it, is full for men; it is a kind of life, ultimate and complete. How is this fullness to be shown? It is not penetrating but it is not inappropriate to think that it might be shown in blessings. This is what is added as an ending to the story of Job. The loss of Job's children is irredeemable. Nor is his suffering made up to him. Job, at the end, could read the blessings right. Those of us who are offended by them seem not to see them properly.

There are questions about the right reading of Job and of other parts of the Bible which these suggestions do not help us with. We are nowadays especially troubled in religion about questions of meaning. Many of our questions about religion are questions about what is myth or meaningless and what, if anything, is true. We will not penetrate much into the issues of religious life, we will not be able to go on much further, unless we see something more about the ways in which words and things can have religious meaning for us. What we will see, once we set aside the blunder about there being a single, basic form of speech, is that there is a distinctive way in which words have their meanings in a religious life.

RELIGIOUS LANGUAGE

Many of us read religious language or listen to it as if it were in a foreign tongue. The life it helps one to live might be ours, we think, if only we understood what was being said. At least we might then consider living it. Without knowing the language, though, religion seems to many of us closed, perhaps regrettably. It occurs to very few of us that, as in the old theme about understanding and belief, we understand religious language only as we have a religious life, not the other way around. Still, if religious language is like a foreign tongue, we should be able to translate it into the language we already know. Or, as seems more likely, if it is not really foreign but only our familiar language overlain, we should be able to remove the overlay and see it as familiar after all. There are a dozen programs designed to do just this: religious language is seen as metaphorical, analogical or symbolical, or perhaps it is expressive, evocative, performative, dramatic or poetic. It is to be translated or simplified accordingly. If only we can find what must be the basic function in it, if only we can see the extrapolations in it, then we will have found our way.

The error here, the presumption, the insensitivity, or impiety, is to suppose that "some" language or some use of language is more fundamental than the religious "one," and that the language used by religious men is therefore a variant, complication or distortion of the basic one. If some use of language, not the religious one, is basic, if the meaning of things is made most plain in the basic use, then the use of language in a religious life can only seem an offshoot of the basic, plainer one. If there is but one way in which to represent, everything significant has to be represented in just this way, any other way only seems to represent and is not really meaningful. There is our basic way of meaning things and other "sorts" of meaning are built up from this; they attach to it or grow out of it, parasitically, benevolent or not. All doctrines of metaphor and symbolism suppose a single basic way of representing things. There is, however, no good reason to think this supposition true.

One bad reason for believing it has, nevertheless, seemed especially plausible. It is based on the so-called observation that religious language occurs "late" in life, and is removed from the most familiar, the most common and perhaps the most urgent uses of our speech. For example, it is claimed that we have to know who our father is before we can call on our Father in Heaven; this second call is then seen as a variant of the first and nonreligious use of speech. The same is said to be true of "bread," "breath," "brother," and of every other word which is thought *to have become* religiously meaningful.

But what is supposedly seen here has not, with assuring sight, been seen at all. Supposed all along is the idea that there is a first and nonreligious use of speech and then, analogically, religious speech later on appears. Think that religious life and language come only late to men and, of course, we will "see" that this is so. But as far as "observation" goes, make a different supposition and things appear much differently. Suppose that there is a religious life, that it is not a variant of another sort of life, that all the language which occurs in it is toned religiously, and then we see that the word "father" is from the first a religious word or has a religious use. It may, for example, be used and only used properly with the honor which one of the commandments enjoins. "Father in Heaven" would then be an intensified use of more familiar religious speech and not at all a metaphor. If a religious life is full, if it touches everything, then in it one has a language of the kitchen, the nursery, the street; there is nothing nonreligious anywhere. Observation, then, will not by itself help us much if ever indeed it could occur alone. Our suppositions about what we represent and how we represent it are more important. We will have to think what arguments can be set out upon these themes.

It is understandable, however, that so many of us think that religious language comes to us late and that it is then derived. It is understandable because we only rarely think how full a religious life can be. We think of religion mainly in connection with ceremonies or holidays, events specially marked off even by religious men, and we are right to see, of course, that the language which is used then cannot be used as everyday language. What we fail to see is the religious everyday, and we then suppose that the familiar in our own day is common to all men. English is English, after all; we have one language and we all speak it and mean what we do in the same way, neglecting, to adapt a phrase, how enormous are the silent adjustments we make to another's speech. With religious lives only partly seen, with the everyday language of religious folk understood well enough for our own purposes, it is an easy failing to think that religious life and speech are but variants of the language in which we live.

A full account of what and how we mean when we use religious speech should comment on scriptural records and the reflections on them which have been made by both religious and nonreligious men. It should explore the significance of rites and rituals, sacrifice and sacrilege, and curses and idolatry. It should consider the claims that creation was accomplished or accompanied by an act of speech, that the names of God are not known or are not to be spoken; that God gives his word to men in covenants and commandments, that he speaks through them in prophecy, and that his word became flesh. It should also reflect on the very profound idea that as one understands what he means by God he is led to God himself. The turns of everyday speech, not only heightened discourse, have also to be understood, otherwise the spread and texture of a life in religion will not have been felt through. Religious language in its fullness is what we have to see. This is of course far more than we can hope to see here in fair detail. Still, a measure of it will be possible if we focus first on the language of prayer. It will be a revealing device to think of the whole of the religious life as toned by prayer, almost as if it were prayer itself, only with the reference of prayer enlarged and its intensity diminished some. This will not be entirely accurate, but the insight it will give us is important and the spirit of the device is not inappropriate.

The words we use when we pray are used at other times as well, and by other people too. They are not private words, even though they are used by us in the most private of devotions. The words have a communal cast. Forms of prayer are more prescribed among Jews, Catholics and Muslims than they are among Protestants. This is continuous with the fact that for these first groups, community is felt to be especially significant. All the groups, however, whether their prayers are prescribed or not, surround the language of prayer with other and less intense language, which has to do with promoting prayer and conducting it, or with conducting themselves in it. Then too, there is advice and admonition about where and when and how to pray, and about what to do before and afterward. There are circles of language spreading out from prayer, spreading as it were to be the language of the whole community. The heart has to be turned in prayer, and in a community of religious men there will be traditions, routines, practices, rituals and instructions by which this turning is promoted, successfully, effectively, or not. We have to be taught to deepen prayer. No matter our later privacies, we start among others, speaking as they do.

It is difficult to isolate the language of prayer from the language which surrounds it. It is also difficult to see what we do with language or what language does to us as we learn how to pray more deeply. Children pray as children do. For the mature, prayer calls for demanding discipline. Through this range, language seems to have different roles or stages of purity which are not readily marked off. Roughly, the major divisions seem to be that we can pray *with* words, or *through* them, or *in* them, as we will see.

Let us think first of prayer as petition or entreaty; it can seem to be the asking for something. It differs then from practical petition mainly in that we petition God. The petition is thereby religious, but not very deeply so. Some prayers can indeed be read as if they were pure petition, the "Our Father," for example. There is first the calling upon God, then an expression of deference, then a declaration of what is in effect a reason for believing that the petition can be granted; then there is the petition itself, and a reverential waiting at the close.

There is, even in the deepest prayer, something like petitioning, which is why it is not appropriate for children to begin learning how to pray by asking God for things. Still, the idea of petitioning is a cloying one and not only when it is petition for this or that, for things we can do or acquire on our own. It is cloying even if petition is constant and is a single petition, say the petition that God shall not withdraw. The pulling impurity of petition is that God is God; he knows what we need and he always gives us our proper bread. He is not under injunction to do what we ask, and to think of asking him for even a single thing seems to some to be undiscerning, even to be near to impiety.

How, more appropriately, can prayer be seen? Another view of it is that we do not *with* words ask God for things but that we express *through* our words our resolution to do his will. We speak not to God or with him but, if to anyone, to ourselves, and God perhaps then overhears, as if we were saying to ourselves that we will do God's will and bear with him as his will is done. Perhaps, though, on this sort of view, it would be best not to think of us as speaking to anyone, even to ourselves. We can think instead of making our resolve through the words of a prayer. Resolve, after all, need not be made first and only later on expressed through words. It can be formed in or through the saying of the words themselves, so that the saying is the re- solving and the words are not a mere carrier of a resolve which is already fixed. They are routes, byways, channels for the shaping or making of resolve. A prayer like the "Our Father," for example, begun as petition, can change us in the course of our saying it. Through even routine prayer, we can move to deeper piety. This can come about because the intent one brings to speech is modified in the course of it.

We bring an intent to every use of speech. We also intend our words to convey our intent, and they fail or not as our instru- ments. But words, it seems, have some substance, some power on their own. It is almost as if there were congealed in them the resourcefulness, the effectiveness and the limits of their past use. When we use them to convey our intent, they also convey the intent which is contained in them—so while we say the words we choose, they in turn have us say what they have come to mean. There is always a strain, though sometimes only slight, between saying what we mean and meaning what we say, and new meanings are born from this intercourse. They are not born, however, without our intent being somewhat changed. What we intend is modified as the words we use make the in- tent we had in using them more definite. No speaking, then, is merely a saying out loud of what we had already said silently within, or even if there is some speaking which is this way, the shaping of intent by words goes back another step. The words we speak fill out the intent we had in speaking and in speaking them. This change is a change in our intent itself. How radical a change there can be is hard to say. But it is not far to move from asking for something and waiting for it to having the re- solve to bear whatever is to come. Such a move can readily be imagined in reciting the "Our Father."

We can, then, move to great piety through the very words of a prayer. The words can do more than carry the meanings we invest them with. With meanings on their own, they can shape what we mean in saying them. Our intent in praying, our resolve before God, can therefore be made in the very course of prayer. Prayer can be the making of resolve. It is because words can do this that religious men have often felt that prayers must be preserved intact and said exactly, jot and tittle, word for word. The power the words have is sometimes said even to be owed in part to God, especially if we were told by him to pray this way. The words of a prescribed prayer are precious, holy routes which can turn us in right resolve toward God. It can be a sacred duty to keep them pure and to instruct others in their use. Said attentively, no matter how often, they can seem inexhaustible in power. The repetition, in fact, freshened each time with new intent, takes us further along a single route and thereby makes for firmer, fuller spirit. There is much to gain in having the words of some prayers fixed and traditional. The only disadvantage comes when those who are learning how to pray cannot get into the prayers or come to feel their force.

But prayer can be even more than a resolve to have God's will be done. There is something unfinished about a man whose resolve is being made. This seems especially the case when resolve is formed through routes which a community, a church, or a tradition provide. Even if their exertion upon a man is tender, the routes, the forms of prayer, are still outside of him. He has not yet got them inside himself, not yet suffused them with who he is and what he means. They help him in having the resolve which makes him more fully a self. But one can go further still. A man can occupy his prayers, live in them, and in doing so be most fully one, without intermediaries or intercession, face to face, with God. One who asks of God attends to him but is concerned as well for what he thinks he needs. One who resolves to do God's will aligns himself with God and is addressed to other things. One who is *in* a prayer, it seems, comes alone to God, is devoted wholly and stands in love to him.

When we ask God for something we use our words as means, signs of what we need and what we want God to do. When our words shape resolve, they are like borders which confine and direct intent and which turn it some. It may come to happen, though, that our words are neither instruments nor a constraint on us—that they come to fit us, that they are a part of us and that we live in them. It is then as if they have no separate meaning of their own but are the silent spirit, skin and posture of ourselves, that we are words ourselves. This is what seems to come about in fullest prayer. Flesh and words, as it were, become one. Can we understand more plainly how this could be so?

Perhaps the idea of "context" will help us. Nowadays, this idea is often used in discussions of significance, though there are grave difficulties in it that have not been set aside as yet. The usual notion is that words are used within a context and that it is only there, or as we see them there, that the words are meaningful. We look to the context and then understand the words. The context is presumably the condition under which the words, rule guided as they are supposed to be, are being used as words. What shows us what the context is, how a context helps us in understanding words, how it itself is understood—none of this is very clear. But perhaps this much is plain: the context is somehow larger than the words; it is a background for them; against it, in it, the roles of the words can be marked out.

Think, then, of using the words of a prayer to ask for things. The context is presumably God and us and whatever connects us together; it also includes our real and supposed need and something of our concern. In short, everything relevant except the words. To see the words in their context then—this is trivial— is to see how they complete the context; it is to see what they do. They are instruments of petition, or, when they are seen to be instruments of petition, it is clear that we are using them to ask for things.

Were it to happen, however, that the words of a prayer change the context in which they occur, they would not merely be inside it. This situation is envisaged in thinking that resolution is fixed in prayer. Abstractly considered, there is no reason to think that words cannot modify their context, for example, when our words change our intent. We have simply to allow for changes of context, one sort of change being owed to the words within it. There is no reason why words cannot have this effect.

But now, having gone so far, since contexts are so indefinite anyway, why not go further? Why not take one or another of these steps? Let words themselves be a context so that we look to them to see the significance of what occurs inside of them? Or, if this seems not bold enough, why not allow the supposition that a context can shrink, so that the words and the context become one? Or perhaps the consolidation might work in this more modest way: the context, except for God, shrinks so as to become one with the words, and then the unity of the words and context points toward God. This last is a good scheme for understanding a kind of prayer, and there are other options too. So far as the notion of context is clear and useful, then, it suggests to us a number of ideas in the search for the sense of fullest prayer. The consolidation of words and context may indeed take us close to the sense we are looking for.

What we have to see is that a man can, as it were, be inside his words and have his words become the whole of him. This is hard to feel because our more familiar views of words, what seem our more familiar uses of them, intrude upon our way. It is easy and sometimes right to think that a man has purposes and that he chooses, shapes and uses words to accomplish them. They are tools of his, and we think of him and them as separate, and of his using them. What he selects, what he shapes and uses are things apart from him. There is a stage of prayer in which a man and his words are joined in just this way. But we can also think of someone struggling for words, not just to find the words which will convey what he has already clear in mind, but for the words to which he can submit himself and through which his meaning and intent are made more clear. Such a man takes hold of words and words take hold of him; each modifies what the other means. This idea of words is also familiar and we can see how it is useful in describing prayer. But now, to go further still, we can think of a man as having been both shaped by words and having mastered them, so that there is no strain between the words and him. He does nothing *with* them, they do nothing *to* him. They are, as it were, part of him, or even more than that, he fills them and they fill him, like a body and its posture, like a cast of mind.

This will have no sense at all if we think that words have always to be distinct from us, so that we use them for this or that or not. Sometimes, they are this way. But they need not always be. We can see this perhaps more easily if we think for a moment about our bodies or our minds. We often suppose about ourselves that we are different from our bodies or that we are different from our minds, as if they were alien, sometimes friendly, sometimes not. Yet we can also come to feel that we fill these with ourselves, when our bodies are disciplined, for example, or when we are absorbed in thought. This perhaps does not happen often or for very long, but it does occur and it can occur with words as well. Words are not mere sounds, so ephemeral that they cannot contain us; nor are we so thick and solid that there is no room in us for the meanings which they have. We can be inside words and they in us; there need be no exertion or opposition, one upon the other. The whole of us can become words and words can become the whole of us. When this occurs religiously, we are flesh-filled words in a single act of prayer. Where we otherwise use language to talk *about* what we isolate apart from words, *in* a prayer, our words are wholly a directedness. Nothing is said with them. We stand in them, whole, devoted, aimed toward God, patient and without demand. This waiting is like petitioning, but nothing definite is sought. It is also like resolve; it is steady before God, there is no turn away from him. Perhaps it is best described, as many are inclined to say, as the fullest love of God.

Love is said to occur in fullest prayer. We are made stable in the awesomeness of worship by our words, but then, with love there, there is nothing one can say with them. Consummate prayer is silent. It can be silent even if words are used and they are overheard by someone else. The silence of prayer has to do with whether he who prays "says" anything and whether he "hears" his words or not. If he does, his prayer is not silent, not pure. He is doing something with the words and is still attentive to himself. In silent prayer, one is, while waiting, wholly directed toward God. Nothing of aberrant self-assertiveness remains. Catholics, perhaps more than any other group, have seen how filled with person prayer can be and yet how little of personality there is in it. Were it sound to speak of essences, one could even say that an act of fullest prayer is in essence no different from the purest prayer there had ever been. Other groups have, of course, seen something like this too. Some, however, hold that one moves in purest prayer beyond all words; others think that purity of devotion, if it will, can bring forth its own words. Words can occur before, during, or after purest prayer. But the differences between these views are minor, turning on minor differences in the understanding of what it is to say a word. Rather, they are minor in being more like one another than any one of them is like the view that in prayer and ritual we are occupied with the symbolical and perhaps not with God at all.

The silence of full prayer is not the silence or lack of self-consciousness of the innocent. Children can be reverent. This may also be true of the uninstructed or the simple. But then their prayers are not likely to be deep. They are not themselves yet full in humanness. There is a discipline to prayer. We have, full and whole, to be turned in love, and we have to prepare ourselves to have this done; we have to learn how it is done. Prayer can perhaps fill us of itself, but only if we turn to it full in what we already are.

Like other disciplines, the discipline of prayer is as dangerous as it is promising. Many have been stunted by prescriptions when routines are too much outside of them. This can be especially true for forms of prayer which are traditional. One is not helped, though, by having no discipline at all. Many have failed to come to maturity religiously because they have been without stabilizing, fulfilling forms. The shaping of discipline is to move into forms which will deepen us but which will be shown at last to have been all along forms of our deepest selves. Discipline, such discipline, has no end. The trials of discipline are, if anything, even harder as we go along. He who is well inside a discipline is more sensitive to what is failure than those who are less disciplined, and he is harsher with himself than with those who learn from him. In the writings of the saints, for example, the confessions are always of their own sinfulness; they, their love, are not as pure as they might be. Discipline is required by what is beyond where we are. It has, however, also to be connected with us where we are so that we can come into it. The bridging points are always difficult to find. Many religious men believe that God himself helps us, that he shows us how to come to him.

The basic discipline needed for prayer is promoted in a community, often by practices of speech. Jews, more than other groups, have emphasized the devotional aim of language. This is perhaps because of the important lesson of Babel, or perhaps because Jews have no singular place to pray, or because the covenant was made with a whole people, not with persons singly. The very sound and shape of speech is important to them. Quakers too, for different reasons, have been sensitive to what we are to say, to whom, and how. For every sect there is a sense of what speech is right, of what is curse and what profane. For some communities, the speech of prayer is perfectly continuous with other speech. For others, it is like a special ritual. In either case, practices in speaking can promote the growth of piety. We should, however, also see that effects can occur the other way around— as we turn from prayer to less focused devotion, the language of prayer spreads to affect the language of our community: what leads us to prayer is changed by the very prayer it leads us to. In the whole of the language of religious men, there comes more and more to be a sacramental cast.

In its intense form, prayer is not the whole of the religious life. Sometimes, it is hedged in, to keep it pure against the profane. If the separation of these two is too severe, however, the wholeness of a religious life is jeopardized. It is perhaps best to think that praying is a nodal point in a religious life and that there are also other though less demanding or fulfilling centers for devotedness. We can think then, not of turning from prayer to secular matters, but of having the singular directedness of prayer diffused, of having the love of God suffuse our lives. For all its awefullness, we will then be steadied by prayer, and in that stance be opened to other things. It is not facetious that a man shall pray before he turns to dealings with the world. If we think that the demeanor of prayer can with less intensity be assumed throughout a life, then the whole of the religious life will have the contours of a prayer. Our aim toward God and our aim through him toward other things, vestments of our prayer, will be joined in a whole life of a distinctive kind.

The language of a religious community, all of it, can in this way be seen as an attenuation of the language of prayer. Since there are grades or stages of prayer, since words can be more or less part of us while we pray, there will be corresponding depths as language is used in breadth religiously. He who petitions God will speak in petition to other men. He who is resolved by prayer will urge devotions in his community. He whose prayer is the love of God will love and speak in love with other men. There is no reason to think that religious speech is any the less versatile or varied than other styles of talk. Its range and tonality reflect the grade, intensity and purity of one's religious life. There are monks who will only speak in prayer. There are also people who cannot bring themselves to say a standard prayer. The first have no spoken language for what is apart from prayer. The second seem to have no language in prayer itself. Both, through the whole of their lives, may be religious men.

Language may be religious even though no "mention" of God occurs in it. This is often true of the language of the children of a religious community. In the learning of the language, they are taught how to address their parents, what they may ask for, when, and of whom. They know what to say aloud and what is to be spoken in whispers. They are told that this or that is forbidden, not dangerous, foolish, or ugly, or if these words are used, they too have a religious tone. Even the shouts of play are turned toward devotedness. The children's language is the language of the religious community, with its scale, depth, range and intensity reduced.

Those who are older will more often mention God or guard themselves from doing so. They see better who they are and how they stand to God. What they see will often show itself in speech. One whose prayer is petition, for example, is likely to greet his friends in a way that God would want him to; he will think whether in all his dealings what he does will incline God to grant his request or not. His speech will be filled with talk of God's name and sake and there will be little dedications at the start and end of his activities. How else would we expect such a man to speak? We are whole and single as being of a kind even if we are not very clear. A religious man is religious, more or less, and the marks of his kind and of his fullness as a man show themselves in speech. One who is a petitioner before God speaks the language of asking, needing, wanting, getting, not getting, worth and gratitude. All this language and what goes with it is religious, even if nonreligious men "understand" it differently.

Men whose prayer is the making of resolve will sometimes speak as if with voices other than their own. Many Bible stories remark that people had never heard such talk before, that in the speech there is authority. It is not then that the words themselves are strictly new; but the filling of the words, their source and directedness, seems not wholly owed to the man who speaks. This, however, is most often a mistake. Resolute men are not possessed. They only seem that way to those who think that God is far away and that he now and then will act capriciously, seizing someone, making him say what the man himself does not intend or mean. It would be better to think that resolute men are shaped by the words which they and others already know, only that resolute men are brought to their resolve by them. If anything in this is magical, it is the words themselves. In them, there are intensities which casual and inattentive speakers do not feel. Even for such speakers, however, there are sometimes shocks. Others point out to them what they have said and they see then, as if it were new to them, that they meant what the words conveyed. A man of resolution takes some of his intensity from the very words he makes his own. He may be in search of resolution, not knowing what he is looking for. Many of us feel that our call will be clarion if only the words will come to us. The words are to shape an intent which, without the words, is too amorphous to be singular. When the words are found, they are felt to be natural, or more than that; it is as if a man himself had been found, or been new-born, and that the words had been given voice and could now say something new.

The language which forms resolution need not be pitched in high intensity. It seldom is, but then resolute men do not otherwise talk a lot. The good caricature for such men is "the silent type," not sociable, but not unfriendly either. Suspicious of talk, as if it were mainly connivance, such men speak when something is to be done, and then they say what it is and are already started in their speech toward doing it. Often, we think of such men as practical. But we can easily see them as religious men whose talk is like what is now called "the speech of authenticity." It is undecorated, not compliant, not often even directed toward others. It is speech in which men mainly fix what they are aimed at and where in that aim they are. The outside of their speech is

159

often most familiar. It seems, especially to them, as if there were no need to say such words.

Men of the highest religiosity seem often to be careless in their speech, but perhaps it is rather that they have the greatest versatility, the greatest self-command in it. Jesus, for example, often responded to critics with the observation that it made no difference whether one said this or that. It made no difference to him—he seemed able to turn his words into whatever shape made love acceptable—but there was a difference for those to whom he spoke. The Pharisees lived and spoke in ritual forms; they had little mastery over them. They thought that one has always to say who it is who heals, and who forgives, and what demeanor one should have before the Lord. In contrast, Jesus and other rabbis spoke as they were moved in love to do, in any words that came; then, as lovers will, they left those to whom they spoke on their own, to do what they were moved to do. One reason so many were concerned to know their words was that the words—important things—were not often spoken so in the law; there might be a hidden sign in them; surely, there were depths. The very words, so Talmudists at least supposed, should be meditated on. Jesus, though, and other men of fullest piety, seemed little occupied with forms of speech. It is as if they had the gift of tongues and that, suitably, words would come to bear what they felt others would be helped to hear—now this style of speech, now that; ritual sometime, sometimes parables, as if the spirit, shaped and steadied, would be the same no matter what words were being said.

Even men of purest faith are not able to stand alone before God for long. The singularity of their devotion reposes from intensity in some single role. The name for such a role is a "vocation" or "call" and here, while speech is religious, aimed through things toward God, it is less intense, more familiar and routine. Kierkegaard remarks that most of us will not recognize a knight of faith when we see him walk down the street. Few will recognize him in what he says. He is not likely to talk of God, nor even to speak in a striking way. A father may offer his child a piece of bread and have his giving-saying be an act of love. There is perhaps no familiar form of speech that cannot be spoken lovingly. Such spirit then does not just accompany the words, as if they would mean what they do, and how they do, no matter whether love is there. It is inside of them, and it makes them, no matter how one takes them up, a service however indirect to God.

In a detailed study, most sensitively to feel for the grain of a religious life, one would be forced to think that there are many uses which we make of words religiously. The sharp, fine questions would be about what a word is, or what counts as being one; what uses are, and what we are to understand by a use of words. The general question which would then remain is why and how the many uses are said to be religious uses of our speech. It is this general question that has been under discussion here. The answer is that prayer is at the center of religious speech, or that what is religious in such speech is most prominent, intense or plainest there—so that all religious speech is prayer or shares in the features which are purest there, or that it surrounds prayer, or prepares for it, or is otherwise shaped by there having been an offering.

This idea of language spreading out from prayer is complicated because prayer is not in everyone the same. Prayer can be more or less pure; we can be more or less inside of it. The simplest clue toward understanding it is to see that all prayer is directed toward God. While attentive to him in prayer, we are sometimes attentive to other things as well. Prayer becomes most pure when all else is left aside; we come more and more to be aimed whole at God and to be wholly in our words, not then meaning any or any other thing. In impure prayer, there are pulls and references to things beside God himself. We stand, as it were, in a position, a posture, where we can point to them, and we are therefore not fully faced toward God. As prayer is made purer, these references are withdrawn, even though the words remain the same. The language is less and less something to do things with; we occupy it more and more and stand, while apart from God, asking, resolving, loving him. The language of purest prayer is the purest pointing toward God; it is wholly pointing. It can endlessly refine the kind of "pointing" one has to do even before he can point to God. This last is a crucial claim.

All pointing, all reference, is as if repetitive. We have to know what we want to point to before we can point to it. We do not, of course, have first to point to a thing for ourselves and then point to it again for someone else's benefit. The reason for this is that our first isolating of the thing to which we are to point is not itself achieved by pointing. One who stabs a finger through the air and then looks to follow it has not pointed at a thing. Referring to a thing, pointing to it, is a deliberate act. One has first to know what is there to be pointed out. This is the sound sense in the view that references are representative. For all references, for prayer too, there has first, then, to be in us a sense for something which is other than ourselves and which has such stability as will enable us to represent it as the object in a referential act. Since it is hard to distinguish in what is other than ourselves the several senses of their otherness, it is no surprise that we have turned devotion to so many sorts of things. We will never understand devotion, though, if we suppose that we first neutrally isolate a thing and then aim our devotion at the thing which we have marked out. No reference is ever neutral, nor is the isolating on which the reference will depend. From the first, for religious men, in their very access to the world, there is a discerning seeking through devotedness.

The image we have to avoid is of a man searching about, isolating kinds of things and then reflecting judiciously which one of them most warrants his devotion and his love. Love is not bestowed on God because we first find him worthy of our trust, as if we decided, in review, that of all the kinds of things there are, it is appropriate to worship him alone. The very ideas of worshiping, of loving, or of devoting oneself to something have themselves to be accounted for; and if religion is a basic way of addressing everything, if it is not derivative from some other kind of life, then from the start, in our very access to the world, there has to be an isolating through devotedness. Worship could not be genuine if there were not something like worship in our very address to what is other than ourselves, and unless that address brought to partial focus what we worship later on in more controlled directedness. Religiously, the only way that God can be isolated from among the things that are other than ourselves is by sustaining or fulfilling our native devotedness. It is not that we first find God and then devote ourselves to him; he is found first through the devotion of our address. What we have to see is that religious men are from the first religious, turned toward things mainly in a loving trust which serves partly to isolate the God whose worship they may later on perfect.

Prayer, then, is the demeanor of such a basic devotedness refined. It is refined first through the practices which prevail in a community, but then it is developed further on our own. Without end, it seems, prayer can be refined. It is a pointing of ourselves, not for someone else's benefit or as a preliminary to saying anything. It is to be in the love of God. What more this means is very hard to say. Still, we should try to understand what it is to be in love with God and to have him unfailingly love us in return.

THE LOVE OF GOD

God is the most beloved of beings. Men have always sung to him. Even the harshest sacrifice is an offering in love. To aim love suitably, however, is the constant trial of religious men. We know now, we think, how reserved men were in the past and how they tried to hide from God. Our own reserve and hiddenness are not so clear to us. It seems that we always fail to love God enough.

God's love of men is said to be steadier than ours for him. From time to time, as the older stories go, God withdraws in anger from the world, but even then he is not beyond all reach. Despite flood, scourge, pestilence and exile, God has been thought to sustain the world. Christians believe that he loves it so much that he sent his son to redeem it. He abides even when men turn from him in infidelities.

Such themes as these about God's love for men and ours for him occur only in the religions of the West. In Eastern religions, there is less concern with passion and person. The mood in consummate devotion is meditative, and in that meditation nothing of the singular person is finally found. There is consistency in this; for if, as these theologies hold, there is no singularity to God, there is also none at last in men. However pure or embracing love is then thought to be, it can join only what seems to be separate, and it is therefore not fully real. It is play upon the surface, beautiful perhaps, but not connective of what is ultimately real. In Western doctrines, on the other hand, as we hold to distinct realities, love is the communion between entities at once most distinct from one another and yet also most akin. It is a way in which some of the basic realities are joined.

How there can be communion between beings as different as God and men is hard to understand. There is a distance between God and us so far as we are distinct; yet in communion the separation is overcome. How does what we understand of God and men lend sense to an idea of love? How does a notion of their communion bear on what we know of them? To answer these questions, we have, for a time, to talk abstractly again, though the love we want to understand is not in the least intellectual. It is an unworldly love which is felt in fullness by religious men.

What our discussion will show is that (1) while we are especially individuated in a present moment, we are even then not wholly self-enclosed; that (2) there is more to us, we have more being, than is located in the present and that, though we are individuals, our potency, our non-present being, is not separately marked out but is merged with the being of other individuals; that (3) we are active in drawing and shaping our potencies into definiteness, but (4) that God helps to strain the being we share with others and to make more individualized potencies available to us; and finally (5) that God does this as a strand in his own activity in dealing with everything there is. In short, our general discussion will lead us to see that God enters into our activity by helping us to continue to be, and that this help of his is given without demand. It is his love of us. Religious men live in special acknowledgment of it.

(1) We are most sharply individuated in a present moment, and it seems hard to see how we are individual at all apart from the press and opposition of a present time. Here and now, we are distinct from other individuals; we border, block and press on them and they oppose us in their turn. One over against another, each of us is separately a one. What there is of us which does not have its being as a present is not so sharply circumscribed. Yet it is we ourselves and not a part of us which is an individual. The "I" who is an individual is not solely in a present

time. It is only that in a here and now we seem most clearly to mark one another out. The "I" who is present, though, enters into that present time; he presents himself, he helps to make a present come about. He must therefore be an "I," an individual, apart from any single now.

But even in a present an individual is not all self-enclosed. We are together with other things as well as opposed to them right now; some communion, some commonness in fact is a condition for the opposition of individuals in a present time. There is spatial commonness, for example, for I cannot cut so deeply into space that the place I make for myself isolates me spatially from all others. My place is a part of a common space, it is not a private or separate space, and my spatiality is not accidental or exterior to me. Even in a present time, then, something of myself must be merged with others and not opposed. Our place is no doubt accidental, as Aristotle claimed; it is accidental that we are either here or there. But it is not accidental that we are spatial and definite somewhere. Spatiality is essential to our being, but our essential spatiality at any moment is indefinite. We are therefore not full round and all complete in a present place. There can thereby be action, opposition and fighting for a place in a present time.

This same spread in the being of individuals is also found in us as we are in a present time. We are not completely fixed in a given moment. Were we to be all enclosed we would have no contemporaries; the present would be our present, each present would stand alone, and there would be no sense in which all the private presents could be, or could be said to be, presents at one time. Our being in a present does not, for all our individuality, separate us wholly from our contemporaries. We are joined with one another in a time from which we each wrest our separate presentness. This nowness of ourselves, however, is not the whole of our present temporality. It is time as inside of us. As along with our contemporaries, we are inside of time, and as we are, we are not sharply separated from the very things we also now oppose. In a present time, then, there is for us something like a space, a place. But as in the case of place, we are spread in presence beyond what there is of us which is definite as here right now. Even in a present, we are not confined, bounded, one and individual only as against others wholly outside of us. We can have contemporaries and can stand against them because we are not through and through cut off from them.

To go further now, what we have to see is that there is also closure and openness for us in that portion of our being which is not in a present time. It will turn out that the closure and openness is opposite to that found in and as a present time: we are more definite, not by opposing others, but by merging with them; and we are filled, not by appropriating temporality, but by being open to and addressing what makes for communion apart from a present time. These last, as we will see, are the marks of love's unworldliness.

(2) We most often think that what there is of us which has not yet been fully shown in a present is a potentiality. It is our ability or capacity, or it is the stuff of it; it is something of us which, while now possessed, is not shown forth just now. In an earlier discussion we saw how difficult it is properly to define "potentiality." Now we need only remember that the notion has to do with us and future moments, and with our lasting through a time. As it was described earlier, potentiality is also connected with ideals or goods and even with the divine. This is as true of classic notions as the one which was suggested here. In Aristotle's view, for example, a potentiality is not only urgent but also directed; both the urgency and direction are affected by our imitating a complete, eternal being, though, for Aristotle, imitating is not itself an activity in which there are urgent efficiencies. In somewhat similar ways the account of persistence which was suggested earlier in this essay sees us as ever wresting presence from an effective, moving time while we aim toward other individuals, while we incorporate the Good, and while we are over against a being, God, who is not himself suffused with transience. To see something now about the love of God, we therefore need not turn away from notions of potentiality. Since they indicate what there is of us apart from passage in a present, they can be of help to us. We need only realign the sorts of things that are thought about in them. Instead of stressing the arrangement which accents present passage and futurity, we can emphasize the connectedness to God. This emphasis gives us,

not "potentiality," but a different notion about the same sorts of things, one in which, not passage, but another mode of activity is prominent.

Our potencies are portions of our being which are not in the present time. Each of us has potent being. It is what there is of us that is more than we are as being here and now. But how shall we understand this potent being of ours? How are we connected or opposed to each other in that of us which is apart from a present? Do you have your potent being and do I have mine? Or is our potent being the same and shared? Is there one potent being which we somehow divide? Neither of these alternatives will do. For if our potencies were melded wholly into one, we would not be individual, nor would there be a way for individuals to come to be. On the other hand, were we all separate underneath, we could not explain why or how we came ever to interact or to have our actions be coordinate. These are the extreme options about our being apart from a present time, and both neglect to see us as active through and through. The best answer to our question is to combine the two extremes, to see that our potencies are merged but not seamlessly so. The idea that there are strands or dimensions in our activity helps us to see that this combination really does occur.

(3) The potencies of individuals are merged, but not wholly so. We, each of us, have active hold on the joined potency, the being of our futurity, and this tends to strain it to individuality. Our non-present being is ours after all; we do not stand wholly in the present and away from it. We reach into the being we share with others, as if to will that a portion of it shall be wholly ours at the future moment we act to bring about. Just as in older doctrines of the will, the suggestion here is that we address and are active in respect to all that will in the future, when winnowed through us, enter in a new present as a feature of an act of ours. This being with which we are continuous and which enters into our activity is, as Aristotle saw, potent and obdurate. We have to seize, shape and control it, and it can overrun our aimed intent. The materiality of it and its movingness explain why it is so hard to do what we will to do and why we so often fail. The explanation is simply that what we have to shape or channel does not yield

itself readily to us. There is real determination through us, real determination by us in making present the stuff of our own futurity.

Stressed into that of us which is merged with others, then, we are not quiescent channels through which becoming flows. Were we to be quiescent, we would control nothing; there would perhaps be no sense in which we could be said to act at all; surely, we would not affect or be affected by what occurs. Our reach into the being in which we are merged with others is indeed part of our activity. But, it is only part of our activity. While we are active in connection with our potency, we are turned toward God as well. God bears on that of us which is merged with others; he also bears on our connection with the other individuals who, like ourselves, are not wholly present now. Were he to have no bearing on us, were we not aimed at him, we would have no steadiness in our address to the potency from which our new presence is made.

(4) Were we not aimed at God and opened to him, we would have no control or only small control on what we do. Potencies would rush through us, here and there restrained. We would be inexplicably stolid. But then, we would hardly say that our restraint of potency was an action on our part. To control, to restrain, to shape our own potency, we have not only to be a channel for it, continuous with it; we have to be dealing with something else as well. It is only as we can adjust ourselves with respect to something else that we can shape ourselves.

This point too is seen in doctrines of the will. What the will helps in shaping is something in which our will is carried out. In Plato's *eros*, in Aristotle's *imitation*, something very like to this is also claimed. Open to my potent being, open to all that will issue into presentness, I can control what is to enter my presentness only if I am also dealing with something which is not itself a potency. My openness to this other thing, my dealing with it, provides for a measure of control upon the being which issues through me into presentness; I affect and control what courses through me only if and as I am turned toward something else as well. God is the being toward whom I am turned and to whom I am open.

We are turned toward God and open to him even if we are not aware of being so. We can, however, be turned or open to him more or less. Religious men are especially sensitive to God's bearing upon us. Others of us are more or less closed or turned away. Still, for each of us, for each thing of the kind we are, God is there. Part of our individuality is owed to our connectedness to him. It is not perhaps, as so many of us think, that God creates us as individuals, though this view is plainly plausible: it is the view that merged with others apart from a present, we are not there marked out or individual but are made to be so by a creative act of God's; it is the view that apart from God we are potential merely, not distinct or real as individual. The sounder view, it seems, is that while there is a respect in which we are individual in our connectedness with God, we are also individual on our own, from our side out, and that our connectedness with God is a correlate in our fullest individuality. God does not create us; he steadies, defines, and sustains us in our being individual.

God, however, seems not to address us one to one selectively. Such a union is affected by us if, as religious men say, we turn or come to him. Apart from such a strand in our activity, God's bearing upon us is through the potency in which we are merged with others. It is as if God were available to us only through the being we share with all others who also act and change. This is something like what theologians have meant by *the ground of being,* as if all that is or could be were sustained by something toward which we might turn. It is also like the more familiar religious themes that God is available to all equally, that he has no favorites, that his providence is for all of us and encompasses us all at once, and that from our side we address ourselves to him. It will also perhaps make clearer why it is that to love God we have as well to love one another and have the love of one another be partly a love of God. How, though, more specifically, are we to understand God's bearing upon us through our being merged with others and how are we to understand our own address to him?

(5) The potency, the being in which we and others are merged, is not cut off from other sorts of things. It has to do with time, and the Good spreads into it as well. As even a Plato had to see, a future flux must be congenial to the forms. God enters into this merged being too, and his effectiveness in it is to promote its being available for presentness. This is the activity of his which is important for this discussion. It is something like the effectiveness of

Aristotle's unmoved mover; it is also something like the activity by which Whitehead supposed that God makes available forms of definiteness—only, instead of being an ideal at which we aim or a provider of forms for us, God serves to promote for us the *what* of what enters into us in our activity, not its form or ideality. It is as if he were a condition for or a partial creator of the making of the world in all of its present times. We have now to see why and how this is so.

If there is more to us than there is in a present, and if it is merged with the more of other present things, then it has ever to be made available to us as we act and continue to be. Why should the merged, the potent, being have to be made available to us? The answer is that we cannot ourselves draw our own potency into presentness. We are not, to be sure, wholly in the present, but so far as we are there, we cannot from there reach into our potential being and bring it into the making of a new present moment. Even as stressed into our potent being, we are not potent enough to bring into presentness all that has to enter into a new moment of our activity. We neither reach into what is beneath a present time and bring it into fresh presentness, nor do we ourselves move from what is not present into presentness. For all our versatile effectiveness, then, we are not adroit or powerful enough to bring together all that finally enters into our activity. If that of us which is merged with others has to come within our reach, if we have ever to take hold of it in continuing activity, it has to be made available to us. Something has to make it available to us. No other claim will do.

Were being in potency naturally parceled out into little wells of bubbling potentiality, there would be no question why the potentialities stream through us. They just would—but then there would be no account of our being together with other things, or of why we last for more than a moment, or of why our potency does not come out all at once. Were potency of itself to be drawn into presentness as we aim toward an ideal or perfect being, perhaps there would be no difficulty with the idea of lasting for a time—but then, it would be hard to see how we are active in shaping potency; potency would be strained by form and the straining would not be an act of ours. Because these and the other options we already understand are unacceptable, we have no alternative except to hold that God partializes potency and makes it available to us—

that what there is of us which is merged with the being of other things is made available for our appropriation, that it is made to come within our reach, and that it then issues into our action because of what we do.

God, then, does not create us; nor does he cause our constant activity; nor does he provide for the forms for things. These are the important doctrines that have been held before. As distinct from them, the claim made here is that God makes available for our individuation that being of our own which is merged with others. He helps us in a distinctive way to continue to be who we are. The question is now, of course, how is all this done. God is not, as it were, our efficient, final or formal cause. Were we confined to this Aristotelian array of causes, our answer would have to be that God is an adjunct to the material cause of us. He makes the stuff of us available to us. How does he do this?

God, it seems, does not divide up the being we share with others and then parcel out pieces of it, one to each of us; nor does he move our merged being closer to us, as if it were a mass, now closer to us than it had been and because of him continuously within our reach. That of our being which is merged with others is continuous with us; it is not made to be continuous, but then neither is it portioned as it is merged, this part mine, this yours, this to something else. Indeed, it is cast as a whole toward presentness by the time which is caught up in it. This thrust of being, though, were it not channelized, would overwhelm us. It always does overwhelm us to some extent; we are always out of balance in the rush of things. But we are helped to take some hold of it by God. God suffuses this onrushing potency—and what we have to hold is that through it, in it, God tries to make his way toward each of us. He tries, as it were, to give himself to us, and in the course of this, the being we share with others is streaked with the singularities of his aims. It is because of him that the wholeness of our merged being is portioned some, or if it is not divided, it is loosened some so that we can take hold of it and make it still more singular as an ingredient in new activity. The stuff of our next moment, the being of us which is made by us to be the substance of our next moment, is made available to us by God or because of him. The simplest way to say this is that the very stuff of life is a gift to us from God.

Each moment of our lives is new. There is more to us, as we

have seen, than is here and now in the activity of the moment. We help to make the moment be; we help to make it come to presentness. Yet time in its urgency is a jeopardy to us. There is something of it that we have to master and appropriate to maintain ourselves as one among others in any present time. Still in its urgent overbearingness, time is not all threat to us. Something of a new presentness is given to us, however much else there is that we have to wrest from it by ourselves. Some portion of the being we share with others, some slight hold on the urgent passing is there for us at each moment's start. It is as though it were a gift to us. It is at least something given. For all the brutality there is in the struggle to live, something of our lives is given to us too. We recognize this sometimes when we are surprised that we are alive. It is as if in each moment there were something of us which is given to us—not the whole of us or the whole filling of our lives, though some theologians have thought this to be true—but only a hold upon the being which we share with others and which is now more singly our own.

Were we to hold that, as we are, we persist altogether on our own, there would be no explaining why anything is for us a jeopardy or why we cease to be. Were we to hold that we have potencies and that these are neatly ours and that they come out on their own, there would be no explaining our coordination with other things and the limits which are mutually imposed. Were we to hold that we do need help as we persist but that the being which God gives to us is not, before the giving, already our own, then with Descartes and Whitehead, we would have to hold that God creates us or helps to make altogether new beings at every moment. Were we to hold that we are helped by having our own being given to us but that we do nothing on our own, then we would not act at all but simply last, and God would be the only active thing. None of these views is satisfactory. It is sounder, though the details of the view are unusual, to say that it is because of God that something of the being we share with others is made available to us and that in and with it we shape the activity of a present time. God, as the saying goes, gives us the life we have.

It has also been said, and I believe the statement is sound, that it is not as the world gives that God gives us what he does. The world, the present, passage and intrusiveness are rude and demanding. Time threatens to overwhelm us in its passage, and at each moment it tears something from us as it goes. Other things intrude upon us too; we intrude upon them in turn, and all resist the others more or less. Peace in the world is a balance of intrusions and oppositions. God's most effective role with us is quite different. He gives us something and takes nothing away, though it may be that through us his own connectedness with other sorts of things is also somehow achieved. He is there for us and without intrusiveness; we can move toward him or not, and no move toward him is opposed by a protective resistance on his part. Giving, being within reach, unresisting, it is right to say of God that he loves all things. In turn, some men turn to him in love.

Men who love God are religious men. They address themselves to God. They address themselves to everything through God, and they try to be with everything in such a way as will bring them close to him. They submit themselves to God, not knowing what will occur but not fearful on that account. Their petition is that, if it be his will, their own wills shall be shaped in him. They also see that all others are sustained by God and loved by him, and that they stand together with these others, bodied indeed together, sons, as it were, of the same giver of their lives. This two-sidedness is inescapable in religion. For no man can love God alone. And no man who loves others is without some love of God, though he may not nourish it or live in it.

God's love for men, for all individuals, is part of his way of being with everything else there is. We are distinct from him but he acts toward us through the being we share with other individuals. Through attentive openness to him, we can help reconcile him with all other realities. God too is an active being, and religious men try to act on his behalf. This is their concern. It is not exotic, or it need not be. All of us are turned to the whole of things in one way or another. Religious men are those who are turned through God and are concerned to have his way with things prevail. In this concern, in their love of God, their lives can be full and filled with blessedness.

Chapter VI

The Types of Men Together

MIXED TYPES AND IDEALS

It is useful to have a catalogue of the kinds of men. By appeal to it, we may come to deal effectively with a variety of men; it is not finally practical to treat everyone as if he too were bent on practicality. A catalogue also consolidates our sense for the sameness and the differences between the kinds of men; it is like a map which shows us, inessentials left aside, how species of humanity really are disposed. A catalogue can also show that in the rich variety of humanness the deepest contrasts are harmonized and that a communion among us persists even amid our differences.

Yet for all its use or sense or other virtues, a catalogue of the kinds of men offends many of us. It seems too plainly wrong or artificial; the *facts* seem to be against it. Men do not seem to divide neatly into four or into any other number of kinds. Then too, if the four that have been set out here are supposed to be *ideal,* it may seem to be far more ideal for men to combine the types, so that the best of men is not of a single kind, but of several kinds, or of all of them at once. As fact or as a set of ideals, then, the catalogue of this essay, perhaps any catalogue, will seem wrong or otherwise inappropriate. Every kind of accusation will be made against it. This is itself an interesting fact. Still, the accusations, or some of them, should be answered to. Let us take first the notion that neither practice, reason, art, nor religion provides an ideal which is demanding enough for men, and that something more than any one of these ought to be our aim. Then, once the demand for ideality has been tested, we can see what the facts about the kinds of men show themselves to be.

Is it enough to ask that we be consummate as men of practice, reason, art or faith? Some of us will, perhaps, suppose that it is not, and will insist, instead, that a man should be more than *merely* one of the four kinds, that he should do more than come to excellence in so *limited* a way, that he should be two or three or all the kinds of men at once. The claim is that we should be philosopher-kings, or king-priests, or artist-thinkers, or perhaps even "renaissance men," practical, rational, artistic, and religious, all equally.

There is an important point in the call for these ideals. No kind of man, however excellent, can give to every sort of thing its rightful due. In being of a kind, men are focused, and things dispose themselves in their concerns. There are fore- and background things, but what is in a background can and should also be brought to the fore. This point is surely sound. It is a mistake, however, to develop it by demanding that each man shall hold the several concerns as equal all at once.

The demand fails to appreciate that in being of a kind, each man is concerned with everything; no combination of the kinds enlarges our concern. More than that, the mistake in the demand is that its combinations are the very opposite of ideal. We cannot be several or all the kinds of men equally and at once, and even if we could, we would not thereby be excellent. We would give to nothing what is rightly due to it. We would be without a focus, without distinctive direction, we would have no task; there would be nothing we are concerned to do and nothing definite could be done. We would be spread impossibly thin. Why is this so?

To be concerned, to aim to do something, we need a focus on

the things we will act upon; there has as well to be something we want to bring about. We therefore cannot confront everything in every sort of way. Divisions are needed; access, routes and ends define the modes of our activity. Were we to lose these, we could not act at all. This very loss of concern, however, this blurring of aim, is what is involved in the ideal of being all the kinds of men at once. It is, of course, not noticed in the commending rhetoric, but it is a sure consequence of the combining of the kinds.

Aim at everything through every access and what are we now to do? Deal with everything through all its parts at once? And to what end? Everything will be our instrument, and there could be nothing we could aim to do. Again, to deal with things, we need entry, instrument and end, and these are all lost to us if we think of aiming equally at everything. To have a concern we must have a focus. Not every kind of thing can be done at once, nor can every sort of thing even be done by us sequentially, as we will see. There can, therefore, be no "genuinely" renaissance men. A renaissance man would be like Buridan's Ass, immobile, unable to enter one of the equally comprehensive ways of dealing with the world. Far from being an ideal, the "truly" renaissance man is a contradiction, and in no sense commendable. We are right, of course, to admire adroitness and adaptability. But we can only find these within the compass of our being of a single kind.

It is no saving to retreat to say that men need not be all the kinds of men at once, but that, ideally, they should equally combine two or three of them—they should be philosopher-kings, perhaps, or king-philosophers, and so on for the rest. But for the same reasons that they cannot be all the kinds of men, even these mixed ideals can have no claim on us; they lose us our singularity. The philosopher-king, so Plato thought, is a philosopher first and then a king, and even then a king reluctantly. Plato does not hold the two on a par. Nor was he able to bring out from within a king a philosopher of stature equal to the regency. A man of reason may concern himself with politics, but he is a man of reason nonetheless. A man of practice may reflect long and seriously, but that does not mean that he has changed his kind or become another kind as well; his reflection simply helps him to be more practical. We cannot, in kind, be divided even into two—reason or practice, not equally the two, no matter how we portion time and energies.

God or mammon, art or piety. We can attend to one inside the other but we cannot be addressed equally to both at once. Multiple concerns are not possible; they are therefore not ideal.

What is ideal is consummate fulfillment in a single kind. A kind of man is a whole man and not a partial one. He takes account of everything in a distinctive way. Because of this, he is ideally enormously versatile. He has to deal with the very things which other sorts of men approach in different ways. For this reason he has to have *something* of their way of dealing with things within himself, which is why it is so often difficult for us to say what kind of man we are, and why we are so attracted to mixed ideals. A practical man can be reasonable, artistic and religious without being a man of these distinctive kinds. He is reasonable, artistic and religious in the way that a practical man can be. It is especially important that we understand this versatility. It will help us see how full, how ideal a kind can be, and how a man can seem to be equally of different kinds even when his direction is really singular.

One kind of man can seem much like another because all the kinds of men take some account of everything. A man of one kind deals in his own way with the things with which another also treats, and he can therefore seem to be the same kind as the other, but perhaps a lesser version of that kind of man. We know, then, what the judgments are: everyone is practical but some of us are excellent, and others of us are timid, or delicate, or too detached in our practicality. But, as we have seen, judgments such as these can be made in terms of another leading kind, and made with the same propriety. To avoid these readings, we have to acknowledge that as men of the different kinds deal with the same things they will seem to be much alike. They will in fact be much alike, but they will not because of this be the same in kind. Men of practice do not occupy themselves with one kind of thing alone. Nor do men of the other kinds. They share the same range in their activity. This is what makes them much alike. Differences between them, however, still remain. These differences are in their ordering of things, in their concern, in what they are concerned to do.

A practical man will reason about things, be appreciative of them, and be devoted to having something done. He will be like

177

the men whose kind is different from his own—but his dealings with things will be practical, and the casts in which he is like the others will be ordered inside his practicality. For him, reasoning is thinking how his practical concern can be achieved in the face of obstacles; his artistry is his efficiency and economy in the use of resources, and his faith is his will to have the concern of practice prevail at last. It is as if reason, art and faith are combined in him in practice, as if they are organized for him under the emphasis of what is needed to deal with everything through his focus on the agencies effective in the course of passing time.

A man of reason will in his own way be practical, artistic and have faith. For him, practice will have to do with turning things so that they can be understood; his artistry is in his imagining what might be or in the elegance or simplicity of reasoning, and his devotion is his persistence in holding that a whole truth can be known. Within itself, reason holds and orders something of the press of practice and of art and faith. The same is true for artists and religious men.

Each kind of man treats of everything. We cannot deal with but a single strand of reality. Even when one strand is placed in prominence, if the others are left too much to the side, we fail to deal properly with even the one which is for us most prominent. If a practical man is not in his own way reasonable, artistic and devoted enough, he will not succeed in practice; if a reasonable man is not industrious, creative and devoted, his thought will be too limited. There are hazards like these for art and faith as well. Every strand of the real has to be dealt with to aim properly at even one of them. It is no accident, then, that men of the different kinds often seem to be, and are, alike. What we deal with demands or explains or in another way underlies the similarities. Differences in our kinds, however, are irremovable. They are as basic as the similarities.

The kind of man we are defines for us an ideal which demands from the whole of us that we deal with everything ideally. No kind is therefore to be commended above another because of its range or the fullness of the life which it provides. What morality the kinds prescribe, what appraising judgments we can make of them, will be discussed more fully soon. Now, we have to see only that as compared with the mixed ideals, only the simplicity of a single kind is feasible, fitting and appropriate. We are to have a life, whole and full, and in the making of it there has to be a single principle. We cannot be all the kinds of men at once, or even two or three of them. We can make the pretense of being them. But then we are near to disarray and deep disunity. Finally, of course, we are not really torn apart. The shreds of our activities are held together in a distinctive way. There is no way for us to escape from being the kinds of men we are or from the demanding ideal which our kind defines.

And how do the facts stand? What do they show? Their appearance can be confused. The kinds of lives seem not to show forth plainly; outlines seem ill defined. One reason for this has just been mentioned: there are similarities between men of the different kinds. Another, closer to the poignancy of our lives, is that many of us, unsure what kinds of men we are, do not take our own lives surely into hand. We do not possess them thoroughly; we do not live them from our side out but, as it were, live inside of them and wait and yearn for a single circumstance which will force to prominence a showing of our kind. If the times do not provide for this, we may adventure to create conditions under which our kind will be shown unmistakenly. We make for ourselves a testing time or testing place, or if we are men of a certain kind this is what we do. Others of us wait for a kind of light, hoping that something will be seen or said which will make us think, and that then the thought, so fortuitous in coming, will show us who we are. Still others of us linger impatient for an inspiration or a calling. For many of us, then, the so-called facts are not plain at all. The facts about ourselves, we ourselves as fact, are not altogether clear. We do not see who we are and how we can naturally take our lives in hand. Even then, however, our unsureness itself has a distinctive cast. Different kinds of men fail in different ways to feel what kinds of men they are.

Our times too, and our places, contribute much to the darkness of the facts. Now and then, here and there, there are established ways in which things are done; there are styles of thought and artistry, religion takes certain forms, and one or another of these may be close to being tyrannical. A man of one kind may be forced to live under the restraint of institutions more congenial to men of another kind. He then lives distortedly, and the facts about his and the other kinds of lives are hard to see aright. Communities, large and small, can restrain us. Be a thinker, yes, but within the restraint of political loyalty. Be an artist, but keep to the prescriptions about idolatry and remember that the censor is the public's guardian. Be a religious man, but serve acceptably, by doing this, not that, and surely not this other thing. Soil may not nourish the seed which comes to grow in it. The species then will not be plain.

The very range and texture of a life, then, our feel for our own concern, and the dominating forms in time and place help to explain why it is so often hard to see the kinds of men and so easy to confuse the kinds. These confusions, though, and our discontent with the lives we have, our failures to find ourselves, and the quality of restraint we feel with the place and time in which we live—the very facts which obscure the fact that we are of different kinds, if we read them carefully—can show us that we really are men of different kinds. The "facts" about the kinds are not so plain that they confirm or disconfirm a claim about the kinds. They have to be penetrated, and when they are, even those which seem most plainly to show that we are not of different kinds, when thought through argue strongly for the opposite.

Each of us is either a practical, a rational, an artistic or a religious man. We are individual as men, and our lives are single too. Our animation toward everything is in order, and it has to be filled and ordered still more thoroughly as we possess our lives. The order of our instrumentalities is, and shows, what kinds of men we are, and no one can be without a kind. We do not come to be of a kind, however, by choice or by an achievement of any other sort. We cannot hide behind the kinds and take one or another of them at our liberty; we are not first men and then, by our design, men of this or some other kind. The idea that we fix our kinds for ourselves is entirely unsound. If we could pick the kind of man that we will be, we would pick in one or another way, but then we would already be the kind of man who makes his choice in that distinctive style. Our kind is native to us and we cannot change. This seems the hard fact, the only option which makes sense, and there is a kind of fittingness in it too.

Still, on this point, many of us may feel offense. We would feel so mistakenly, however, if we supposed that, really, one kind of man is better than the rest and that, therefore, everyone should have the chance to be of the best kind. Since no kind is better than the others, there is no ground for the thought or feeling that in being of this or that kind one is thereby naturally debased. There is no hierarchy in kinds. Nor should we even feel that choice, freedom, or preference have been foreclosed. Within the kinds, we have all the room there could ever be; there is no wider place for anyone.

There may, however, be still more unease for us about this point, a last unease. It is expressed in the feeling that if we had only been born in a different time, raised in a different place, trained in a different way, or had different opportunities, we might have been a different kind of man. If this is what we think, there can be no full response to it; it plays too loosely with *if* and *might,* and it is a view we should not hold. The hardest answer to it is simply that if we had been trained differently or had different opportunities, we might have had a different job or otherwise behaved differently, but that we would not have been different kinds of men.

Many of us have not had the opportunities that permit us to exhibit excellently the kinds of men we are. We are nevertheless still men of our native kinds. We have all known displaced men whose lives are skewed—a lawyer who is natively an artist, a teacher who should have found a fuller field for his practicality, a salesman who is a philosopher, a mechanic who is a prophet. Whatever the cause, none of these has been able to exhibit his concern in a preferential way. And it would be impractical or a failure of other kinds to insist that if they had been real poets, real philosophers, real prophets, they would have found or made a field for their pure pre-eminence. It is right to rail against a world that does not lead us to excellent exhibitions of our kind, or which does not allow for them. Something may be done because of that. But it is wrong for us, and wrong in us distinctively, to rail against ourselves because we are the kinds of men we are. It despairingly confirms for us who we are, and the futile self-preoccupation keeps us from any excellence.

Inescapably, a man shows what kind he is. A rational man walks and talks and sees and serves all out of his rationality, but he may not have been able to become a scholar or teach in a university.

The Four Faces of Man

No one supposes that he can have any sort of body, as he chooses. Nor should we suppose that we can have as dominant a mind, or sensitivity, or will. We are not thoroughly plastic. We have natures, natively, as men of certain kinds. The type of men we are is fixed in us; it is fixed for us, and then it is refined and perhaps fixed still more steadily. Parents, home, community, friends and enemies, economics, peace and war and accidental things shape the filling of the kinds of men we are. A man may live in an era when he can exhibit his concern excellently; he may also live so that his concern is not enhanced. He may have its exhibition distorted, and throughout his life, feel ineffective, have his vision clouded, or be ill in spirit, dragged in a kind of sadness, frustration and despair. Each man is of a kind, and as he tries in his own way to take himself in hand, it may seem to him that the kinds war within him for the leading place. Some men never seem to settle who they are. Still, in the course of things, whether we will or not, we show what kinds of men we are and how we are properly to be judged. Others may see who we are, even when, sadly, we ourselves do not. Judgments of us can have finality.

THE VARIANCE OF MORALS

The concerns of the kinds of men always overlap. By design or incidentally, men of one kind sometimes support the aims of other sorts of men. It often happens, though, that concerns collide; we get in each other's way. Men of the same kind often clash, of course, but we know how their opposition is to be judged and reconciled. Practical men oppose one another practically; one or another is finally more effective and gets his way. Men of reason are intellectually opposed; such reconciliation as they can have is made out thoughtfully. A common concern measures the misalignment of men who are aimed in the same way. In the opposition of different kinds of men, the case is not so clear. Intellectuals judge politicians harshly; the judgment of practice upon reason is, in turn, no less practically severe. Art and science, faith and reason, state and church—these have often been opposed to one another, and their overlap will always be somewhat strained.

What sort of judgment can be made in these cases? What sort should be made?

We know, of course, what judgments are most often made. One kind of man indicts another for not having his own virtues to the full. An intellectual may say that a politician is not reasonable enough, that what is being done is blunderous and makes no sense. He may see a man of practice as a man of reason, only not so reasonable as himself, too coarse or busy to give himself to finest thought. Or, he might with less reason suppose that while a man of practice is, in kind, different from himself, reason is nonetheless the proper measure of what a man of practice—for what any kind of man—may do. Such primacy of kind, as we have seen before, has been claimed for each of the kinds in turn. There is a virtual anarchy in the claims. Just as reason can claim reasonably to know about the sense of everything, so practice can rule practically on reason and all else; art can in its own way be an arbiter, and religion can everywhere distinguish sacred from profane.

What troubles some of us in this is that the knowings, the rulings, and appraisals and the judgments seem weighted too one-sidedly: the concern of one enterprise is offered as the ideal for all the others, and the others are not given due regard as separate and distinct. Can we not be more impartial? Can we not stand aside from the distinct concerns, view them neutrally, and then, in that neutral stance, rule, or know, or appreciate or judge the oppositions and competing claims? Many of us would like to think that this can be done. Can it be? How? The most important suggestion about achieving such judgment is that we shall appeal to a sovereign morality. Whatever may be the kinds of men, we are all, or so it is supposed, moral beings, and we can therefore all be judged in moral terms. Morals, then, with terms and principles of its own, might be thought to apply to everyone and to all the kinds of our activity. Is this a sound idea? Is there one morality in whose terms all actions are properly appraised?

It would be most remarkable if there were. We would have to view the sovereign morality in one or the other of two extreme ways. On one option, the principles of morals would have to be independent of all our concerns. Practice would have nothing to do with them; they would not be among the special objects of knowledge, nor would they fall within art, or even enter our concern for God. Clumsy in practice, we might then still be exact in assessing the rightness of an act; we might otherwise be fallible and full of error but still know what it is good to do, and this same soundness could be ours no matter our lack of grace or our deep impiety. This is, of course, an extreme. But it is one we have to consider in thinking of a neutral but sovereign morality.

The most pungent critique of such a view was made by Bernard Shaw in *Major Barbara*. There, Andrew Undershaft's son, Stephen, claims that his birthright as an English gentleman is to know the difference between right and wrong. Undershaft, whose own birthright was different, exclaims in response:

> You don't say so! What! no capacity for business, no knowledge of law, no sympathy with art, no pretensions to philosophy; only a simple knowledge of the secret which has puzzled all the philosophers, baffled all the lawyers, muddled all the men of business, and ruined most of the artists: the secret of right and wrong. Why, man, you're a genius, a master of masters, a god! At twenty four, too.

but then,

> You are all alike, you respectable people. You can't tell the bursting strength of a ten-inch gun, which is a very simple matter; but you all think you can tell me a bursting strain of a man under temptation. You darent handle high explosives; but youre all ready to handle honesty and truth and justice and the whole duty of man, and kill one another at that game. What a country! What a world!

What a view!—that morals stand at all remove from the separate aims of practice, knowledge, art and religion and that, of themselves, the principles of morality are coercive, plain, applicable and appropriate. All of us have been too tormented in our judgings to bear with such simplicity. Nor is the view more bearable when it is weakened by supposing, for example, that even if we do know what is surely right, those who are not scoundrels can, for anything, sense surely whether it is wrong. Strong or weak, hard or soft, there is no saving for this view. It will not work, it is not true, no quality stands outside all appreciation, and religions are not judged in moral terms. A morality independent of our concerns cannot be effective on them; it cannot be applied to them, it cannot be a part inside of them, and it cannot define for us an individual responsibility. A morality which is neutral by being apart from our concerns is too far from where we are.

But neither will the other extreme view do—that our defining concerns are not distinct and that all of them reach toward achievements which can be appraised in the same terms: practice shall be good, knowledge shall be good; art and devotion too: "good" shall mean the same for all, and in each case it is a moral term. No more the good, the true, the beautiful, or the holy, but instead the Moral Good which stands beyond all these and leaves aside the taint of their specificity. This is our second option. As extreme, it too turns out to be unsound.

The unsoundness is that an overarching Moral Good is not the good of anything, nor is it good for anything. Effectiveness is the good for practice; deep knowledge, the truth, is good; fine works of art are good; and fullest piety. These goods, however, are defined within our distinct concerns. A Moral Good which is still more general adds nothing to any one of them. It is without their definiteness, and it has no meaning of its own once their specific meaning is withdrawn. It is in fact empty. All it shows is that concerns have some very general similarity, that the different kinds of lives are each, though in their own ways, whole and unified. It would be a great mistake to take this general similarity as a most general unity, to name it the "Moral Good," to say that all our concerns are aimed at it and that they enliven it distinctively. A Moral Good, so vaporized, would not be found in anything. Effectiveness can occur, truth or beauty can, but not the Moral Good as such. It is, as it were, too good to occur, too good to be the good of anything. A Moral Good beyond what we are in distinctive ways to do? We cannot make one out, nor can we see that such a good could have a claim on us. It is a phantom, figment, illusion, a nameless and false God.

Both extremes fail. There is no neutral moral principle. None has ever been isolated because there is none to find. Accounts of the good are, all of them, specialized, and it seems but a provincialism of modern philosophy to suppose that ethics is an independent enterprise. There are indeed as many kinds of ethical theories as there are concerns and kinds of men. What is the Moral Good?

In what is it to be found? One sort of theory claims that it is in the consequences of action, in promoting happiness for the greatest number and, in the long run, in creating an excellent state, or in something else which is just as practical. Not there? Well, then another theory is that it is in the intent to have all we do legislated by a ruling reason so that our lives are consistent and fleshed to fullness by our rationality. Too austere? Then still another sort of theory sets the Moral Good in the fullness of feeling, with vitalities unemasculated and our energies streaming undeterred from their single source toward the consummation that is natural for them. Finally, there are a hundred formulations of the view that we are moral only as we live in the sight of God, as we are guided by the injunctions he provides for our providential good, or as we imitate the life which he himself is said to have shown us that we can have. Be a man of practice, of reason, art or faith—there is a morality appropriate for each of these concerns, and it is an old harshness, an old error, and an old insensitivity to insist that the excellence of one kind of man is properly the standard for all the rest.

Moral theories are not independent of our concerns. Each kind of theory can see something of what another will see, which is why ethical platitudes are shared by all the views but filled in differently; it is also why each, provincially, can claim that the others are versions of itself. Still, the theories differ and there is no neutral ground on which they can be judged. This, however, does not mean that there are no demands, no injunctions, no obligations, no duties, no ideals. There are, but they have to do with the kinds of men we are and with the fullness of our lives.

Each man, within his kind, is aimed and his life is measured by everything there is. He is measured in his activities by his blunders, his ignorance, his insensitivity or impiety. These, not merely what men say, are the deepest judgments. We hardly sense their depth when, as many moralists seem to do, we think of single acts, as if they were self-contained, and then ask whether the act or man is good or not. Acts are not so insulated; judgments are not so trivial. The configuration and fullness of a whole life has to be taken into account to understand and appraise an account. Is it right to lie? Well, what do we count as a lie or as dissembling? In what context, in what concern, is it accurate to say that a man has lied?

Does a politician lie when he says that he will not be a candidate? Did Socrates lie when he said that he did not know what virtue is? Does one lie when he tells a story? And what is the failure if we do? Leave our concern aside, fail to see how our failures affect the whole of us and our activity, and the very meaning of our acts is lost. It is no wonder that so many men have been driven to demand that we go beyond moralities, that we transform our values and become larger men than morals enjoin us to be. Take account of distinct concerns, and acts vary in their kind; judgments vary in their meanings too. The variance in morals cannot be undercut or overcome. Assessment still remains. For the larger men who sense the reach of their concerns, the assessment is that they and others always and always have to fail.

No matter how we try, we fail. We fail because we do not bring to the whole of things that distinctive unity for them which our concern enjoins. No one has his practice endlessly effective. Knowledge is never without taint or partiality. Created beauties are never fine or large enough, and saints know best how far they are from God. In what we are concerned to do, the deepest judgment of us is that we fail and have to fall far short. The case is not quite the same for "single acts," but it is petty comfort to take note of this. What we think of as single acts, cut and portioned from our lives and from the fullest range of things, may here and there be excellent. In them, we see perhaps as fully as we ever will the excellence which our concern enjoins. It is not empty, then, to say that we always fail if there is a sense in which single acts can be judged as fine. In one or another act of practice, in the understanding of a single thing, in a single work of art or a moment of loving closeness, an excellence can occur in small. This is possible. But none of us is ever satisfied with it. We may recollect it as a golden moment, treasure it, try to recapture or repeat it, to have what occurred in it come about again. But for none of us is a single act the whole life. The demand of the concern of our kind of life is what defines us morally, and on that demand we fail. It cannot be wholly satisfied.

It is a cliché of most moral theories that we cannot be required to do what is impossible. This is perhaps sound for single acts, if demands can be rigidly circumscribed. But if we reflect on a concern which defines a life, if we reflect on the demand that such a concern provides, it is shallow, niggling and perhaps profane to think that we are enjoined to do only what is possible. What we are concerned to do is, in different ways, impossible. And it is precisely because it is impossible that our concern fittingly sets its demand on us. There is one demand for all the men of a kind. There cannot be as many demands as there are individual men for whom different things are in fact possible.

What we have to do is fix the effectiveness of the world forever; or we have to know everything, or make a harmony of the whole of things, or, without reserve, love God and the world. We cannot do these things to the full. We cannot do them individually, and even though the demand of our concern leads us to join with others who share the same concern, it is not sure that all of us who are alive now, acting together, can do all that we are all concerned to do. Our communities have to extend beyond our time. Only then will it be possible to have done what we are concerned to do. No one of us alone can do it. But all of us, at all times together, fix that fullness as a possibility. It is not impossible that there be a concert among individuals. It is not impossible for a single principle of knowledge to provide for the intelligibility of everything; nor is it impossible that time and God shall be unities for all else. These could not define concerns for us were this not the case. In the course of history, then, through an indefinite course of inquiry, in continuous creation, and in a vast catholicity of the world, all that we are enjoined to do can be brought about. Since no one of us can do this on his own, we are each failures. And our failures remain ours even if they are redeemed by the supplement which the efforts of other men provide. We cannot help but fail. Our concern is larger than our reach. Still, without relief, we are enjoined by its demand.

The failures that we and that other kinds of men also have suggest finally the sense and fittingness in our unavoidably one-sided judgments of other men. As we have seen, we often judge other men in terms provided by our own concern, whether they share our concern or not. There are no other terms for us to use. Still, there can be something sound in the practical ruling that the intellectual is not practical enough, or in the claim that this or that piece of practice has not been well enough thought through. The soundness is that intellectuals have not taken account enough, even in their own terms, of that strand of things with which men of practice are most concerned; or, for the other case, that practical men have not been attentive enough to that feature of the real through which men of reason know. The idea is that even though we cannot judge in terms other than our own, we can judge fittingly if we are ample and flexible enough. We can sense whether different sorts of men in their dealings with the world provide place enough for that configuration of the real which defines the excellent for us. We can say whether our shoe is pinched, whether our sight of things is obscured by them, whether our creations are being soiled, whether we are more or less obstructed in our move toward God. The point is that we cannot indict others for failures of the kind that only men like ourselves can have. But we can indict them for failing in their own ways to allow for the making of the kind of excellence we are concerned to bring about. This is a failure in their own concern.

To bring out this point again: practical men do not fail in the way in which men of reason do. Men of reason are caught in ignorance, error and unclarity. These, in turn, are not the failures of religious men or of the men who live in art. Still, looking to the other sorts of men, we can be right to criticize them in our own terms. Our indictments will be inappropriate if we think that other kinds of men have failed in the ways in which only men like us can fail. Meant properly, the charges acknowledge that there are differences in kind. The charges are that men who are different from us fail in their own enterprise by not providing for an excellence of the kind that we are concerned to bring about. We can testify to such failures. Our rightful charge, formed in our own terms, can signal a failure in the distinctive acts of other sorts of men. To be excellent as the kinds of men they are, their enterprise must leave a place for us. They cannot finally do what they are concerned to do unless our concerns also have full reach. The restraints and limitations which occur in our concerns because of them mark a failure on their part. As men of a distinctive kind, then, out of our own concern, we can testify to there being failures by men of other kinds. Read narrowly, as the accusation of our kind of failure, the testimony is ineffective, inaccurate, unfitting and inappropriate. Read widely, in the fullest flexibility provided by our concern, it can be a sound criticism of the other kinds of men. There can, of course, be fitting commendations too. The final sense, however, for such commendation or complaint depends on how all the kinds of men can fit together. How do the kinds of men fit together? What is their community? Is it true that for each of the concerns, the others are a supplement? This is the final issue to which we have to turn.

COMMUNITY AND CIVILIZATION

Peace or patience between men of the different kinds is fragile. It is likely always to be short lived. The wars between us need not be severe, but some adjustment, serious or not, is always going on. Men of one kind, out of their concern, intrude upon what other men are concerned to do. Each is concerned for everything; their concerns therefore overlap, and here and there the ways of each will not be coincident. When the intrusions occur, one kind accommodates itself to the demands of another; perhaps both realign themselves a bit.

These are not the ways in which many of us view the settlement of the great conflicts between the kinds of men—the wars between science and religion, for example, or between reason and feeling, politics and art. Many of us think that these wars occur when men of one concern invade the domain of another, as if there were distinct provinces and that the trouble comes when, by malice or mistake, one kind of man intrudes upon another's place. Neighbors will live in peace, we think, if each tends to his own property.

Unfortunately, the issues are not this simple. Our lives are more complex, they are richer and more poignant than this view of limited concerns will let us see. We have seen this point before. To show it now in still another way, we can reflect on the ambiguity in the so-called settlements of the great wars.

Take, for example, the conflict in the last century between science and religion. A central contention in that conflict was the import of the Darwinian doctrine that species evolve, that in a discerning understanding of evolution, there is no need for notions of purpose or plan, good or bad. This doctrine has since been seen to be so partial and unclear that no one is now a Darwinian in the nineteenth-century sense of that term. In the late 1800's, however, and in the early part of this century, there was sharp opposition between the scientific and religious accounts of man's origin and development. There were dozens of special questions, and there were partisans on both sides. Were we to have untrammeled inquiry? Is not inquiry sound and proper only when it is guided by what has been revealed as true?

How did the dispute end? Indecisively, superficially. Mainly we got tired of it, and scientists and religious men seemed soon to go about their concerns in much the ways they had before. After a time, it was as if there was little to learn in the contention, and little to proclaim. It even seemed tasteless to continue the contest, and there was something like a political adjustment too. A third kind of man will often try in his own terms to mediate disputes between some other two. Many began to say that really science and religion are concerned for different things: if scientists will only recognize that there are things beyond their province, and if religious men will only read certain passages in their bibles as metaphors, everything will be just fine. Quiet came. The issue was said to be one of trespass. Talk seemed to make the boundaries clear. Both enterprises could, it was said, have a separate place.

But no one in science or religion was satisfied with this for long. The demands of the two concerns could not be so readily confined. Whatever is special in man's connectedness with God, different from the other animals, has still to be set out; then too, the great commonalities of our kinship with the other animals have also to be seen. The whole of things, not a part of them, is to be understood; and yet there is also a religious demeanor in which men seek an access to the world. Neither concern could, or could for long, bear with restraint or confinement. The so-called settlement which satisfied the public did not satisfy the men who were concerned.

They withdrew a bit. Their public statements were ambiguous. Where they seemed to divide science and religion, what they really did was modify, not the reach of their concerns, but the style in which they developed them. They less and less defined themselves as those who were opposed to one another; there were permissive accommodations about what could be taught as theory but not as fact; and there were gradual changes in the institutions which support the two concerns, so that collisions, even contacts, were more and more reduced. Nowadays, there is a safer distance between the two, though apprehensive attentiveness still remains. There will be a flash of controversy now and then over the import of the Heisenberg Principle, for example, or the cause or history of Jesus' death, or on some issue about the conception of a child. The distance is now so great, however, the barriers and separations so firm, that a consuming opposition between the two is not likely to arise. The last opposition was settled superficially. It led to a change in the accents with which concerns are pursued; accustomed styles were modified; new styles have been developed since that time. The concerns themselves, however, for all of the contention, in reach and aim remained throughout unchanged.

Except when there are great tyrannies, this same withdrawing, this same developing of new styles, occurs whenever men of distinct concerns conflict. None is satisfied or content for long to have the range of his concerns restrained. The accommodations can occur because men of the different kinds do not in fact contend through the whole of the ways in which their concerns are followed out. Distances on matters of contention, seeming overlap elsewhere—this is the formula for peace and patience between the different kinds of men. None really shortens his concern. One may hedge here and there for a time or bide awhile. But then this is perhaps the practical thing to do; it may be judicious; it may be the pace at which the drama is to be played out; it may also be deemed the course and contour of God's will.

Men of different concerns cannot finally live together by dividing up the whole of things, by having one kind concerned for one part of things and having the others take care of other parts. How, then, can the different kinds of men be together? And how can they be together so that each can come to fullness in his kind? Is there a single community which can appropriately contain all the kinds of men? Is there an overarching context in which, jostling perhaps here and there, men of each of the kinds can still find a fulfilling place for themselves? Men of the different kinds can, of course, live together in different communities. But is there a kind of community which is ample enough to contain all the kinds of men so that, with none subservient to another, none dominated by the others, all the kinds can come to fulfillment in their concerns?

The answer to this question is "no." The reason for it is obvious: communities themselves divide as to their kinds. There is a political community; there is a community of inquirers; there is a culture or the community which a culture provides; and there is as well a community of believers, a people chosen or a church. Each of these is broad enough so that all the kinds of men can be found inside it. But then, under the restraint of a community's being of a kind, there are restraints on some of the kinds of men who live within it. Their concerns are made subordinate to the concern which defines the community and which the community mainly supports. No kind of community is able to accommodate equally all the kinds of men. The widest, the least constraining context in which men of the different kinds can be together is a civilization. A civilization, as we will have to see, is not the same as a community.

The most well-known claim about community, and the most strident one in modern times, is made in behalf of political communities. The claim—an Aristotelian view—is that a state aims at the highest good, and that the goods of all other enterprises are contained within the good at which the state is aimed. Benign, though, as any state may be, its concern is practical. It is not defined by a concern for the concerns of men who are not practical, and if the aim of a state is regent, all other concerns are ruled as subordinate; their proper place is defined within the aim of practicality.

Sometimes a state's practical restraints are harsh and heavy. Even when they are not overbearing, there are strains which make it difficult for an impractical man to fulfill himself. A practical man may, of course, oppose his state. But he may also live easily within it. His opposition or acceptance is direct. This is not the case with men of the other kinds. Nonpractical men are always at a tangent to political communities. Where, for example, a practical man can say "my country, right or wrong," a man of reason never means this with unqualified practicality. He strains as he is political. The best he can do is make politics an instance of a rational principle. Instead of allegiance right or wrong, he may say that in the long course of things it is wisest to have steady commitment to a political community, even if the practice of a state is not invariably appropriate. He means, then, not my country right or wrong, but "this country, even if its practice is unsound just now, because it is wisely aimed and will be sensible more often than not, or sensible about the most important things and for the longest period of time." So it is that reason qualifies the cast of reason's politics.

Furthermore, it is only in a special sense that a man of reason sees a state or country as really being his. Is a scientist, for instance, as a scientist, a citizen of America or Russia, or of any place? If there is a community natural to those who want to know, it will not be a local state. It will be a community which spreads across the lands, across even the time which measures the span of nations. One who is in this community will only incidentally be part of a state. Perhaps a man of reason should not be said to be *in* a political community at all, but to be *at* one, or to be living in the place of a political community. His loyalty to it will be owed to his seeing that it has principles which he thinks are sound. He is loyal to principles first and only then to a state which incorporates them. There is no reason politically to suspect such loyalty; it is as sturdy as the principles and as sturdy as loyalty of any other kind. Still, men of practice may suspect it of being fragile and too qualified. He whose loyalty depends upon what he thinks could change his mind. Deeper fibers, so men of practice feel, make for the sturdiest nationality.

Inside the lineaments of a state, then, there may be harshness for men of reason, or there may be fair room and flexibility. Knowledge may grow and even be supported in a political community. But this does not mean that a state is the first and arching community in which men of reason and other men come to fulfillment in their kinds. There can always be, there have always been, constraints by a state upon men who are not practical. Such men are only awkwardly inside of one.

Religion too, to see another case, is not bound to place. Christianity has no boundaries. Missionaries claim a higher right to go from place to place. And men who are born or live in different countries may be Christian, Jew or Muslim, and are not lesser members of their church or people because of that. The "problem" of reconciling church and state is genuine and insoluble for

those who think that there is a church and for those who think
that there is a state. See religion as a matter of singular and
private conscience, so that there is no community between believers, and there is no church to intrude upon a state. See a state
as an anarchy, or as a tissue of routines in which there is no
restraint or coerciveness, and the state has withered, gone, and
nothing will coerce a church. But where there is both a state and
a church, the two will here and there collide. Neither, in their
reach the same, fits without constraint inside the other.

It is the same for those whose community is a culture. A culture
is the unity that a sustained and embracing sensuosity provides.
It is never wholly now or in a place. Men who live in widely
different places feel kin to one another in their sensitivities, or
they feel it a failing if they do not. Nations may accent a culture;
each has its laureates, and story and stone may mean more in one
place than another. But no nation owns a poet. Even buildings,
bound to place as they are, are part of the culture of the world.
A culture spreads, even if the leaders of a nation protest what they
think of as foreign decadence. The art within a nation has a claim
to being saved even when the nation is victim in a war. Culture
and nationality are only uneasily confederate. It may be that
politics as politics cannot adjust itself to the impressiveness of a
culture. But then, neither can a culture be restrained within a
political community. As the saying goes, it may simply flower there.

Where practice is regent and where it coerces to community
other kinds of men, then, more or less, they will feel those constraints and cannot with good fullness do what they are concerned
to do. A man of reason is a citizen only incidentally, not first a
citizen and only then and afterward one who tries to find the
truth. It is the same for men whose "natural" community is a
culture or a church. Such men may live uneasily inside a state. A
state presumes to act on their behalf in doing what a state can do.
Men who are not practical, however, are not aimed at what a
state is concerned to do. A state, therefore, always misunderstands
them to some degree. It always channels them toward ends for
which they are not concerned.

There would be constraints of other kinds if men of different
kinds had to live within a community defined by what a man of

reason knows, or by what a culture makes available, or by the devotion of religious men. Now and then in the course of history, one or another of such communities, on small or larger scale, has come about. With it there have always been poignant losses for men of other than the regent kind. Within one community, channels, preference, pace and aim are defined by regency. We are not so plastic that all of us can readily find and fulfill ourselves inside their course. We yearn sometimes for a different time and place and plan or think or dream or pray for a different time to come. In doing this, we measure our own communities.

A single kind of community, then, cannot provide for fullness in the lives of all the kinds of men. Each provides constraints, and not all constraints are constructive ones, barriers that call upon us for those enriching exertions which make for excellence in our kind. It must, therefore, be that the most ample way for men of all kinds to be together is in a loose unity, not one of overarching singularity. Such a loose unity is constituted by all the kinds of communities together. It is a civilization. A civilization is not itself a kind of community. It does not rule on what shall be inside of it, or how. It is one thing—made up of, and made up from, all the kinds of communities, and it will be full or not if the communities which make it up are themselves enriched. Because there is no singular basic reality, because several realities are equally basic, no kind of community excellently embraces all the kinds of men. But because all the kinds of realities can be together, there is always a civilization, and there can be one of excellence. What we will have to see is that, though men have always to be either practical, rational, artistic or religious, if they are excellent, they are also men who are civilized. They will be civilized by their practice, reason, art, or by their spirituality. This—the final claim—follows from this essay's widest view of things.

Everything there is, in whatever way it is, whatever kind it be, is together with everything else. There is an interplay between all the kinds of things. This is no novelty, of course. But, as we have seen, there have been different views about the ways in which what is real is together, and for each of these, there are correspondingly different accounts of men and their communities. The view of this essay is that the togetherness of all that is real is not owed to one reality, but that there are several realities, all fundamental, each contributing to its unity with the others and urging their togetherness with it. Accordingly, the argument is that there are different kinds of men, different kinds of communities, and a loose togetherness of them all.

This togetherness of communities is owed basically to the fact that each kind of thing is together with the rest in a distinctive way. Individuals, for example, confront not only one another; they have also to take account of the Good, and time, and God. These enter into the being of an individual and each, as also distinct from individuals, ever confronts the individual with the task of incorporating it still more. This is true in turn of each of the kinds of reality, each in its own way. Each gives of itself to the others, but then, as something on its own, it also stands apart, confronting the others with the task of bringing into fuller unity the realities that are distinct from it. The connectedness of realities, then, is in their interplay, it cannot be owed to one of them alone. It must instead be that the final unity of things is owed to all of them, to their being loosely together—at once, so to say, preserving the different ways in which the different realities make for themselves unities with the rest.

In a less abstract context, the analogue of this same claim is that there are distinct sorts of communities, and that in their different ways each of these takes account of all the rest. Practical men can deal practically with men who are not practical; men of reason can come to understand men different from themselves; artists appreciatively deal with others, and religious men turn in love to everyone. No one of these kinds of men, however, can on any ground urge his prominence above the rest. The fullest togetherness for men is to have practical men be practical, but to be so effective in their practice that they provide practically for there being men of different kinds. It is to have the community of men of reason so finely reasonable that they understand that there are men who are in kind different from themselves. The finest artistry will be in appreciating that while artistry enters into everything, there are features in things which are as basic as the one which defines the art. Then too, the gentlest patience and most reaching charity is to go out to men who are not of a religious kind. These, then, are perfected not merely in the place grudgingly given to them by a wary practice, but on their own, as enterprises as basic

197

as practice itself. This openness to the independence of other enterprises is the mark of civilized practice. It is the mark of civilized reason too, as we see that reason has its fullest reach into things when practice, art, and religion come from their sides and in their own ways to the excellence which they define for themselves. The same is true for art and religion.

In an excellent civilization, then, all the kinds of men, all the kinds of communities, come to the fullness of their own concerns in their own ways. This can be done. Nothing in the whole of things forecloses our coming close to excellence. Nothing, though, insures that such excellence will have to come about or even insures that it is likely to. In the interplay of the kinds of things, in the interplay of the kinds of men, conflicts and adjustments have always to occur. No one kind of reality can be fathomed through, none can be entirely and forever controlled, none can in appreciation be fully taken in, and none can be in fullness loved. We, all things, stand somewhat apart from things different in nature from ourselves, and we have ever to adjust them to ourselves and adjust ourselves to them. It is not an odd accident of the world that no state endlessly endures, that no philosophy is completely true, that no work of art captivates the whole of things, or that God's way with the world is not altogether done. We are ever actively in interplay with other realities. Finally, that means that we are never fully excellent as men, nor are we civilized enough.

Both as individuals and as kinds, some of us fail less than others do. None of us, however, no kind of man, can claim to be finer or more important than the rest. Each kind is a supplement to the others, and each needs a supplement. If there are men of but one or two or three of the kinds, they cannot deal fully with what is real. A man of each of the kinds deals with the whole of things, but he deals with it in accent, through one rather than another of the basic realities. He thereby minimizes certain features of the real. They are subordinate to the reality for which he is concerned; and in that lesser place they affect the adequacy of his aimed hold upon the whole of things. It is therefore only as all the accesses to reality are followed through that the good in our dealing through any one of them can be assured. This openness to there being concerns other than our own, this demand that there be ways other than our own for dealing with the world, is what we should finally see. It is not merely, for example, that if we are really practical, we will be as reasonable, as artistic, and as religious as practice allows; nor should we see merely that it is not in fact practical to suppress reason, art, or faith. What we need to see is that civilized practicality demands that there be kinds of men who are not practical but who are in different ways intent upon dealing with the whole of things.

A civilized man is a kind of man; he is either practical, or a man of reason, art or faith. He is one who while being of a kind, feels or understands or appreciates or lovingly acknowledges that there are men who are in kind different from himself. Just as we cannot stand behind the kinds, reluctant to be one or another of them, neither can we transcend them, passing through them to stand apart from the focus which a kind provides. Within our kinds, however, if we are effective in practice, if we are deeply reasonable, finely artistic, or religiously devoted, we can, in our own ways, feel for the partiality of our own way of dealing with things; we can sense that there can be ways other than our own for taking hold of things. Excellent men of the different kinds can bear with one another, understand something of one another, appreciate one another, or enrich one another with their love. Though we are each focused men, if we live fully in our kind, our focus permits us to acknowledge that there are men whose kind is other than our own and that they are as important as we are in the whole of things. Nothing stands higher than the excellence of effective practice, deepest understanding, finest art, and purest love. No one kind of man is better than the rest. As we move in our kinds to become civilized, we can find this to be so.

Chapter VII

Review of Theses

—————

Arguments have been given throughout this essay to support the theses that were set out at the very start. Reasons having to do with everything from an infant's speech to the cosmos as a whole have been cited to show that men divide into kinds, that the kinds are equal, and that none, in general, has preferential place.

These reasons have occurred in different contexts, in abstract discussions, and in comment. They are scattered, and I have not brought them together to enforce their persuasiveness. There is no way now at the very last, briefly but convincingly, to reorder these reasons in a large and singular argument. What can be done instead is simply to review the theses and to cite the most important of the reasons that argue for their being sound. These may then bring to our recall the other and supporting points which make for the sense and strength of the claims. The arguments, in summary, then, of weight themselves, will also be reminders of other arguments. It may even be that they will suggest how an exposition of these theses might have been ordered and expressed had it been aimed at a single sort of audience.

The theses in general are that there are four basic realities, that we are ever active, and that we deal with all of them. We deal with all the realities through one of them, aiming to have them all unified by that one, and, as men, we are different in our kinds as one or another of the realities is our aim and access to the rest. Since the different realities are basic, the different kinds of men are equal to one another in the basicness of their kinds. This parity among the kinds of men remains, despite the variety in the kinds of our activities.

Now, more specifically, the theses are that:

(1) *Each man is essentially bound up with every other sort of thing.* The main support for this claim is in reflection about our nature. We are naturally either self-contained or not. Were we self-contained, we would not need to act; there would be nothing we would need; nor would it be possible for us to enhance ourselves. Action or activity are not accidents for us, though. We have to act, and if our being is ever to be in activity, we are in essence connected with whatever sorts of things define an activity as ours. All the basic sorts of things, not one or two of them alone, have this defining role. We are, for example, not *merely* natural beings who superstitiously suppose that we are aimed at something supernatural, nor are we divinely created beings who incidentally suffer in a world. We persist, know, create and worship, and all of our activity shows the cast of these heightened endeavors. There is no basic reality, then, which is not in some way constitutive of our activity. We are concerned with all of them.

(2) *Though the range of concern is the same in all men, each of us channels his concern.* We are concerned with all the realities. There is, however, something or other that we are concerned to do—and that specific end is consonant with our being concerned with everything. The consonance comes in our being concerned to have everything unified in the way in which one of the basic realities can unify the rest. Each of the basic realities provides an access to and a supervening unity for the others. Each, therefore, can define a concern for us. In turn, each of us must have a concern. Without one, we would be so ill defined that we could have no

centered, aimed, or appraisable activity. We would not be individuals at all.

(3) and (4) *There are four ways of focusing concern. They are the focus of practice, the focus of reason, of art, and of religion. Each of us is, therefore, either a practical man, a man of reason, or of art, or a religious man.* The four basic sorts of realities are Individuals, The Good, Time and God. Each of these provides an access to the others, and each can unify the others too. Each, therefore, can be a focus for our concern, thereby defining us as being of a kind. Since there are but four foci and since each of us has to have concern, we are, so to say, either basically men of practice, of reason, of art, or of religion.

(5) *We do not deliberately choose our focus, though we have some choice about how we will show what kinds of men we are.* Were we to choose to become a certain kind of man, the achievement would be the result of a distinctive activity, and we would therefore already be men of the kind who engage in activity of just this sort. All our activity bears the mark of kind; we cannot stand inactive behind the kinds and then act neutrally to make one of them our own. We are therefore natively of one or another of the kinds, and we cannot change the kind we are. Within its vast flexibility, we have all the freedom a man can have. It occurs within the meaning giving restraint provided by a kind.

(6) *We may be unsure about what kind of man we are.* It seems plainly a poignant fact that few of us have come "to know ourselves." The reason for this, it is often said, is that we are deep and self-evasive, hard to reach and hard to find. This is not altogether sound, for we are not hidden or recessive finished selves. The difficulty is rather that many of us find it hard to find ourselves because we have little self to find. Much in our activity is not action and it is only in our action that we are. The fuller the action in our activity, then, the fuller we are, and the more readily we can be seen, by others and ourselves. Crises help us to come to such maturity. They are a jeopardy to our aims, and discerned jeopardies provoke us to do more.

(7) and (8) *It is a mistake to think that everyone is the same in kind. But each of the four kinds of men exhibits traits which the others also have.* If there are four distinct kinds of men, it will be a blunder, an error, or a failure of taste or love to take

everyone to be, in kind, the same as ourselves. Those about us may indeed be the same, but then not everyone is the same. We are led to this mistake because of the great similarities between men of the different kinds. These are owed to concerns being formally comparable, and to our all having to deal with the same things, everything. Still, despite the formal similarity, despite the conformity required by the things with which we deal, differences in kind remain. They are in the mode of our activities, in our ordering of realities, in the differences owed to our access into things, and our final aim.

(9) *There are no more than four kinds of men and there are no mixed types.* There are but four basic realities, and the basic realities define our kinds. There are therefore four and no more kinds of men. Nor is an amalgamation of the kinds possible. Such juncture would make action impossible. Since we are essentially active, we could not be at all were the kinds to be combined in us.

(10) *The four kinds of men are equal in value or importance.* Support for this last claim is in the argument that four sorts of realities are equally basic, that none is pre-eminent, and that none could be by itself, without the others. Reality itself, then, is the ground for the equality of the kinds of men. There is no stronger ground than this—but then, critics of this book will question whether the portioning and wholeness of reality have been soundly set out in it.